SEAN TOBIAS AMBRIZ

A captivating account of the toll combat takes on Soldiers (mentally and physically). Compelling lessons in leadership that SFC Ambriz learned as a young Soldier and later demonstrates as a sergeant leading Soldiers.

—*Colonel Robert English, U.S. Army, Retired Former Chief of Staff, U.S. Army Aviation and Missile Command*

A story of war, courage, commitment, and tragedy, SFC Ambriz shares his love of country and fellow Soldiers. The triumphs and tragedies of war unfold with every turn of the page. He shows how teamwork, preparation, and leadership overcome all obstacles.

—*Colonel (Retired) Ronald Isom, Former Group Commander*

A gripping and honest glimpse into the joys, grief, accomplishments and struggles of a leader in combat! Ambriz, highlights the exceptional performance of his team members and unit leadership throughout the book. A MUST READ for today's leaders, especially Lieutenants!

—*Colonel (Retired) Donald Gentry, Former Chief of Operations, Multi-National Force, Iraq*

Sit down, buckle up and prepare for a full sensory deep dive into a real Soldier's combat experience of America's longest war. His writing style grabs you from the start and pulls you uncomfortably and unfiltered into the realities of asymmetrical combat. This should be Required Reading for all military leaders!

—*Major Spencer Beatty author of The Art of the Brief*

Sean is the real deal. A proven combat leader. Ambriz's stories of combat had me tossing hand grenades in my sleep.

—*Bronston Clough, former Army Captain, Ranger Instructor, and author of Get Tabbed, Ranger Patrolling Guide, Special Operations: Advanced Patrolling, Land Nav: Basic to Advanced, and Tactical Checklists*

A testament on the realities and recovery of war... Ambriz's writing style pulls you in and makes you feel as if you are there... if you are looking for leadership combat lessons learned or simply to understand the Afghan war this is a MUST READ!

—*Former Captain Lee A. Kind, Doctor of Strategic Leadership, and Military Leadership Author*

Ghosts of the Valley is a must read for anyone that has served in the middle east during combat or in a peace keeping mission. It was a riveting emotional trip back into the middle east for me as a veteran of the Gulf War... SFC Ambriz provided his unique inside perspective to modern war through his personal experiences during combat operations... Ambriz provides details that only someone that walked in his shoes could provide... his friendships... his ups... his downs... his losses... and the life changing decisions he made in a split second to save comrades and protect his allies. I recommend any military person or family member to read this documented account of his experiences in effort to better understand what someone goes through and must continue to bear that serves this great country in combat!

—*Chief Warrant Officer 5 (Retired) Harry Hobbs, Phd, DBA, Ordnance Corps Hall of Fame Inductee 2013, Bronze Star Recipient during Combat Operations 1991, SGT Audie Murphy Inductee 1988, SGT Morales Club Inductee 1985*

GHOSTS of the VALLEY

"The best life insurance policy for your Soldiers is better leadership."

PREFACE AND MEMOIR
BY
SEAN TOBIAS AMBRIZ

SERGEANT FIRST CLASS, UNITED STATES ARMY
MILITARY POLICE CORPS

Printed in USA by Mentor Enterprises Inc.

PUBLISHED BY
MENTOR®
ENTERPRISES, INC.

123 Castle Dr. STE C, Madison, AL 35758
256.830.8282
admin@mentorinc.us

1st Edition, 1st Printing, 2020
ISBN-13: 978-1-940370-45-3
ISBN-10: 1-940370-45-0

DEDICATION

To the men and women of Second Platoon 984th Military Police Company "Punishers," Second Platoon 127th Military Police Company, 3rd Squadron, 61st Cavalry Regiment, and 2nd Infantry Brigade Combat Team, 4th Infantry Division whose extraordinary courage in the face of great adversity inspired me to write this book.

A portion of the profits from this book will go to the 1LT Tyler Parten Memorial Fund.

While all the stories in this book are true, some names, identifying characteristics, and other details have been changed to protect the privacy of the individuals involved. In some cases, composite characters have been created for the purpose of further disguising the identity of individuals. Finally, in some instances the author rearranged and/or compressed events and time periods in service of the narrative.

Ghosts of the Valley

Table of Contents

AUTHOR'S NOTE

We all have our own internal monologue or commentary that seems to run through our head daily. Stressful events along with challenging days tend to make this voice louder and inescapable. For years, this voice got the best of me and I was not sure how to suppress it. Mentors of mine told me ways to combat it and some recommended I write about it to help others.

So, why am I writing this book? What is the purpose of it all? Well, I wish I could give you that answer, but I have no idea. I am still uncomfortable about the idea of publishing a book exposing my life story and experiences. Critiques scare me because I am an emotional person who cares about what others think, mainly because I try too hard to make others happy. My personal feelings aside, people needed to hear some of these stories. Those in the military need a better understanding of our military police capabilities. Although these are my experiences, I only wish to tell the story of my brothers through my eyes.

Some were worried that re-exposing myself to some of these events in such detail could set me back, but the thing is, I see these events every day in my head. Nevertheless, in order to help myself reconnect with some of the situations, I had to exchange stories with some of my old friends I served with, watch videos from deployment and re-open some doors I wasn't ready to go through.

A small part of me wants to place the details on paper to help with my healing process. A bigger part of me wants me to tell the stories of gods. My friends, those I served and fought with, to me, were gods and you couldn't tell me otherwise. Every morning they laced up their boots, met with death, and punched him in the face. In doing so, my duty is to tell stories of their heroics. To enlighten the younger generation and prepare them with our experiences for their ultimately inevitable face off with death.

—**Sean Tobias Ambriz.**, US Army Military Police

FOREWORD

I initially met the brush fire that was SGT Ambriz in early 2011 when he was assigned to the unit. Sadly we had different mission sets for deployment so we trained in separate venues. In April of 2012, SGT Ambriz was actually assigned to my platoon. It was the first time where I was assigned a soldier and before I got to take my platoon, I had to get a brief on his exploits, which was a impressive list of feats indeed. Having already spent thirty-six months as a platoon sergeant, I was admittedly hard to impress. The logic broke down quite simply to me that the great SGT Ambriz was a naturally heroic SOB in combat. Unfortunately, the unit had no war to fight, and I needed leaders who could operate in the calm of peacetime. After hearing the stories that sounded so extreme they seemed fake, I was concerned that the great SGT Ambriz wouldn't be a peacetime capable character. Additionally, I was concerned that since everyone held SGT Ambriz up so high, he might have drank a little too much of his own Kool-Aid.

Now before I go any further, it's important to note that SGT Ambriz's accomplishments are well documented, and as the military police corps goes, well above average. The military police corps suffers from some identity crisis problems. Amongst some commanders we are only perceived to be good for guarding the access points of the bases. Amongst other commanders we might only be good for enemy prisoners of war. Both missions are well within military police capabilities but are not the entire breadth of our capabilities. Military police soldiers, much like the other occupations in the military, find their mission changing in accordance with the operating environment. On top of the standard military police mission set of convoy security, police station advisory roles and key leader engagements MPs found themselves cross training based on the unit they were assigned to. In this manner MPs became far better trained than before and those who embraced these cross training opportunities were provided expert instruction from specialists in the craft. SGT Ambriz benefited greatly from these cross-training opportunities.

Flash forward to the garrison environment and I had a choice to make, how to deal with the fabled Ambriz? The way I saw it, I could fill out my application for the Sean T. fan club and wait for the T-shirt, or I could find out just how good he really could be. As appealing as a Sean T. fan club shirt was, I decided to choose the latter. Ambriz strolled into the office to meet me for the first time, no doubt having already heard just as many stories about me as I had heard about him. So, I decided to kick the hornets' nest and see what came out. I began our conversation with an extremely blunt commentary which dulled down to the fact I didn't care about how much of a bad ass he was in combat. I needed a peacetime leader and if he couldn't write memos, awards, counseling or NCOERs, then his combat exploits wouldn't save him and I would treat him the same as I would any other incompetent leader.

In true Ambriz fashion, he basically responded with "hold my beer." Not verbally, but with his actions. Not liking to be called out after years of so much praise, Ambriz decided to train. He trained himself in the administrative functions, coached a warfighter competition team, and sought opportunities to improve. Even if those opportunities consisted of driving his POV into an active wildfire to aid emergency services with the evacuation of an old man who didn't want to leave until "The Price is Right" is over. In the end, after murdering some of his memorandums, counselings, and NCOERs, Ambriz turned out to be just as good in peace time as he was in war. Even though I never signed up for the fan club, Ambriz is one of the most decorated soldiers I have ever had in my organization.

The stories you will read in this book will provide a couple of valid insights. To the standard MP, what you will see are the fruits of seeking out cross training and the survivability that comes with it. To the non-MP, these stories serve as a big thank you for the cross training received as well as a hint of what a good MP is capable of. To the civilian, these stories might help the understanding of why so many veterans come back quieter than they left, and are a little more wary of crowd and loud noises.

—**Jon M. Waterhouse Jr.**, US Army Military Police

INTRODUCTION

"The most important thing I learned is that Soldiers watch what their leaders do. You can give them classes and lecture them forever, but it is your personal example they will follow"—(General Colin Powell). I first met SFC Ambriz when I took company command and he was one of my platoon sergeants. I have heard mixed reviews; "He is too soft on his Soldiers" or all he does is complain about every mission that he is given. The SFC Ambriz I came to know and really admire was a much more complex individual and Soldier.

The 18 months that SFC Ambriz worked for me, I quickly realized that he poured his heart and soul into his platoon. He did this to the point that his marriage suffered and once he left work, he was exhausted. The other part of SFC Ambriz that people mistake about his dedication and demeanor is that his heart and soul never left Afghanistan. He was still in a god forsaken country that took his closest friends and his most valued mentors. As a decorated soldier, you would never hear him talk about his two valor awards, but you would see the effort that he put into his soldiers, to ensure they were never in that situation. The thing in his life that means the most to him is his wife Aimee. Aimee and SFC Ambriz have not had the typical marriage and have faced more challenges than most. Not being able to have kids or not having the time to connect, really brought these two together.

As you begin to read this book, you will soon understand what events have developed SFC Ambriz to the Soldier and leader he is today. I can't think of another person that I would want by my side in a fire fight then SFC Ambriz. He always gives 100 percent and he expects the same from his leaders, peers, and subordinates. "Nearly all men can stand adversity, but if you want to test a man's character, give him power." (Abraham Lincoln) SFC Ambriz is a soldiers' leader and is continuing his journey to reach his full potential in the United States Army.

—**Angel Mendoza**, US Army Military Police

PREFACE

The crucible of combat, which has been studied for hundreds of years, rests upon a foundation of deep human factors that develop leaders. Decisions forged together by many great leaders are immediately disregarded during first enemy contact as the fog of war permeates the battlefield.

A soldier is wounded and bleeding out, while the enemy moves closer for the kill. You look down in time to see the soldier's eyes glaze over as he struggles to hold onto his life. *What do you do? Do you order your squad to flank the enemy and possibly incur more loss of life? Do you sacrifice one soldier's life to ensure the rest survive? Or, do you hold your ground and try to save his life while possibly jeopardizing the entire squad?*

In combat, decisions must be made in split seconds. Unfortunately, some of those decisions can cost the lives of those charged with completing the missions. If you make a choice that ends with the death of a soldier, how are you supposed to feel? Imagine having to face these decisions at the young age of nineteen and try to accept it when leaders say, "I understand and it's not your fault." Is it possible to accept that sort of minimizing? I stand before you today, ten years later telling my story even as I continue to try and make sense of it all.

In combat for the past 20 years, found itself reverting back to it's primal stages. An enemy who was behind in technological advances utilized it's rich combat experience and overall tenacity to try and stand on the toes of the great American fighting force. Young leaders volunteered to lead this generations countrymen into combat with little to no combat experience and only the images of the world trade center as their motivation. With a constant microscope, social media globalization, and neutered rules of engagement, I watched my leaders consistently make life altering decisions while maintaining mission focus. I watched as others made greater sacrifices under harder decisions and with each experience I gained from those I served with, I placed the next brick of my leadership platform.

Stay awake!

1

Stuck Between a Rock and a Hard Place

November 2011

Kunar Province, Afghanistan

"Wake up!"

Melton's warm breath spilled down onto my face as he waved his flashlight in my eyes, and shook my bunk. "Sergeant, wake up, we got a call, they want us to grab Explosive Ordnance Disposal (EOD) and head out,'" Melton said as he walked out of the room. Completely disoriented, I sat up on my bed rubbing the sleep out of my eyes while trying to wake up. The room was still pitch black, but muffled sounds of the squad waking up and grabbing their gear could be heard as they made their way to the door. Since I already slept with my uniform and boots on, I took the next few minutes to compose my ritual meditation before a mission to collect my thoughts. It wasn't so much a religious tradition for me. It was more of a self-awareness attitude to prepare for the next possible physical transformation of life: Death.

EOD? I thought, *I guess that means something or someone is blowing up tonight.*

EOD were the crazy sons of bitches who liked to make things go boom and were the sadistic shits who got a hard on for disarming live bombs. It was 2 a.m. on a beautiful chilly Afghanistan morning when we were woken up to escort EOD out to a possible improvised explosive device (IED), which is a roadside bomb. Our squad was on quick reaction force (QRF) that night, which meant we needed to either help someone in need or be the fast maneuver element on the battlefield for the commanders on call.

As an MP we were known to be "Of the troops, for the troops," and our job was to maintain law, order, and discipline. In a garrison environment we conducted law enforcement operations and ensured the safety of all military installations. In a deployed environment we were the commander's multipurpose unit that was able to conduct response force operations, area damage control, route reconnaissance, cordon and search, critical site security, and convoy/personnel escorts.

That's why I love being an MP. We are some of the most professional law enforcement individuals, but at a flip of a switch, we could be asked to be turned into a killer. I enjoyed placing others' needs before mine and helping solve problems during law enforcement missions. However, tonight's agenda included turning the enemy into pink mist.

Getting ready for this job was no different than my Wall Street peer counterparts. Throwing my vest overhead and onto my shoulders was the same as putting on a business suit. Picking up my rifle was my briefcase equivalent. Walking outside, the cold crisp mountainous air hit my skin and burned my lungs. Climbing into the passenger seat of my truck, I grabbed my headset while shoving a half-eaten protein bar in my mouth. Once I could hear all communications, I looked at my driver, PFC Garcia, and asked what the situation was. Barely awake, Garcia looked at me and briefed me with his crusty morning breath that battalion spotted multiple individuals, two miles down the road, digging. First off, digging in Afghanistan, especially at 2 a.m. usually meant they were planting an IED and not serving their local community by planting fichus trees. Second, screw them for having me wake up this early. Kids. From reconnaissance surveillance, all we knew was that there were multiple individuals digging on the road. No information regarding vehicles, weapons, or deliberate ambush sites was noted. So, our job essentially was to go out there, slap their hands, and tell them, "No!"

No one said much in the truck and just subconsciously flowed through their routines checks. During last-minute preparations, Garcia skimmed the truck for deficiencies and ensured we were not going to break down or be left stranded. Melton and Doyle, my gunners, prepared the ammunition and lubed the weapons ensuring that the one thing that separated life and death worked for us. I always brushed over their work and doubled down on the inspections while also conducting radio checks to ensure we had communications to the outside world from our vehicle. Most importantly, we all would conduct checks of our snack bag ensuring we had enough chocolate and goodies to last us three days. *Womens' menstrual cycles had nothing on our eating habits.* Although these checks were tedious and repetitive, I tried to keep in mind that my soldier's protection was always my number one priority. They were all I cared about. During a firefight, every ten seconds I would scan my soldiers head to toe, a hundred times, because as a leader it's no longer about my safety.

Once we pushed off base, the EOD Noncommissioned Officer in charge—or NCO—Staff Sergeant (SSG) Reyes, coordinated a plan to maneuver to the individuals on foot in hopes of getting a better view of the situation as opposed to driving into a possible ambush. Our drivers were instructed to drive with their night-vision goggles on and their headlights off so that we would not warn the enemy of our approach. We stopped on the road 500 meters away, turned our vehicles off, and dismounted all team leaders and additional personnel from the trucks. Exiting the vehicle, I had a much-needed stretch and adjusted my night vision goggles. The rest of the squad started to march in a line formation toward a village to our right, in an effort to mask our movement rather than using the open road.

It was an eerie feeling walking up and setting up an ambush on the enemy—usually it was the other way around. Ninety-nine percent of the time we were the ones reacting to contact and being caught off guard. As we walked into the unknown territory of this small village, I skimmed every corner, window, and doorway. We looked for anyone who would be watching us or maybe even warning the Taliban of our arrival. Nothing moved in the village, which seemed like an Afghan version of an old haunted, western ghost town. It wouldn't surprise me if it was actually haunted—especially with the amount of people who have died in this area over the course of history.

By the way, I don't know if you've ever personally used night-vision goggles, but they're not as cool as you'd think. Ambient light is used to enhance surrounding visibility, so when you have poor moonlight, like we did on this particular night, it sucks.

Extra care went into trying to be silent in our movement, even though every step we took brought the little sounds of loose rocks and dirt shifting under our feet. Looking through the night vision coupled with the low luminosity of the moon made depth perception extremely poor. I tried to utilize my other senses in the absence of vision by focusing my attention on the sounds around me and controlling my breathing.

Once we exited the village, we maneuvered parallel with the river, toward the digging site. Using the sound of the river to conceal our movement, we halted and consolidated 150 meters from the target. Kneeling behind a dirt berm, I scanned the road and surrounding area but could not see any movement with the poor lighting. *I need to get closer.* With the leaders huddled up, Lieutenant (LT) Pleasants, my platoon leader, split us into three groups. SSG Castellanos, my squad leader, was in charge of the base fire support team. Essentially, he would have multiple automatic weapon teams to lay down suppressive fire from an elevated position overlooking the digging site. My lieutenant would take an assault team and maneuver as close to the road as possible and to prepare, if needed, an ambush on the enemy digging site. He instructed me to grab my M-14 Enhanced Battle Sniper Rifle and maneuver to a position of relative advantage to support both teams while reconnoitering for additional enemy fighters who may be concealed in fighting positions.

Once all teams were set, SSG Castellanos fired an illumination flare into the air, exposing the battlefield in a bright light and spooking the individuals, who we could now see were holding weapons. Before any shots could be fired, two individuals who were digging dropped their shovels and ran down the road away from us. Both individuals had their weapons slung on their backs and because of the rules of engagement, we could not fire upon them as they were not presenting a threat to us. The other enemy fighters near the road took off up the hill and with the poor moonlight, our night-vision goggles were having a hard time displaying a visual of them through the dense rock. It would not have mattered anyway, because the enemy fighters were too fast in this terrain. With the flare flickering overhead, I scanned the dense rock terrain for any movement of enemy fighters. When you mix things like sleep deprivation, anxiety, and stress, your mind starts to develop mixed signals and creates patterns of sounds and sights that aren't really there. *I seem to have lived in this box.* Just as I started to see movement, the flare burned out.

Moving up to the road, we assessed the threat and figured the enemy got spooked and departed from the area. Now, we just had to sit back and let EOD do their job. "This will be fast," said no one ever! During my time in the military, every soldier who was not EOD seemed to bitch about how EOD takes forever to do their job—myself included. Though, after watching the teamwork that night, I had a new respect for how they conducted themselves. But, let's be real… you'd take your sweet ass time too if you were dealing with a live bomb.

It was deathly silent as we used our flashlights to scan for wires and freshly dug dirt, which would indicate a bomb. Irregular height differences in the dirt road could show us if a pressure plate was present beneath. Six of us stood on the road looking at the digging site for any signs of possible bombs that might have been planted. There were no holes or signs of loose dirt, so to me, it didn't even look like they started, and we might have come just in time to foil their plans.

"Ha-ha," SSG Reyes giggled, looking down.

"What are you laughing at Sergeant?" I asked.

"We're standing on top of the IED."

"I'm sorry, come again?"

"Yeah, these boys are getting good at covering up their tracks. Can't even tell it's freshly dug dirt," he said as he pulled on a wire from the side of the road.

"No, see, you're standing on top of an IED. I'm going over here. This is why no one wants to hang out with you guys," I said as I walked away.

I hated dealing with IEDs. They were not used as often in Afghanistan as compared to Iraq, but they were still haunting regardless. Standing at an IED site or watching vehicles pass in front of you spiked anxiety. You always wondered how it would feel if it exploded in your face. *How fast would it be if this blew up right now? Would I feel anything? Would I bleed out slowly?*

Standing in the road, off to the side, I looked out toward the river. I started to hear baby rocks and small pebbles rolling down the mountain face behind me and onto the road. I looked back at SSG Reyes, who was tracing the wire of the IED up the hill and before I could see what he was pointing his flashlight at, everything got real.

"Don't you do it! Put it down!" SSG Reyes yelled.

Staring up the mountain, three flashlights were trained on an enemy fighter who'd crawled out of a hole and was standing 10 feet above us on a rock ledge. Both of his hands were at chest level and he was mumbling words with his eyes closed. His left hand was curled, with his palm facing away from us in a praying manner; his right hand, he clinched a Russian-made grenade.

Shit! Where did he come from? What the hell is he holding?

Raising my sniper rifle up, 10 feet below from his left, I had a clear shot of his right arm, with the hopes that if he reached for the grenade, I could disable him long enough for SSG Reyes to tackle him. With my night vision flipped up on my helmet, I looked down the scope of my rifle using the moonlight and the light from the flashlights to acquire my target. It was dark and I could hardly acquire my target with my weapon swaying back and forth. My M-14 rifle weighed roughly 11 1/2 pounds and was 35 inches long, which meant that I was having a hard time trying to keep it steady while aiming at a target as small as an arm, even from only 10 feet away. No one was sure if the pin on the grenade was pulled. If we killed him, the grenade could roll down to us. Everyone was screaming at the enemy fighter. It was so chaotic—I couldn't even decipher the different commands being thrown at him. Sweat was trickling into my eye and my arms were letting me know my rifle was getting heavier by the second.

SSG Reyes, who was about 7 feet from the enemy and walking closer, kept demanding him to stop. The enemy, on the other hand, had other motives that night as he reached for the grenade. *It's about to get hot.* I fired multiple shots into his right arm and upper torso. Four others also engaged as well as one of the machine guns. As his body was collapsing, multiple rounds continued to penetrate him until he completely laid flat on the rock face.

After the firing ceased, I walked up onto his position to secure the grenade, while checking the surrounding area. The aroma of blood filled the air within 5 feet from his body, which was riddled with so many bullet holes, that he resembled a block of red Swiss cheese. When I shined my flashlight over his corpse, the sight of hot steam could be seen exiting his bullet wounds as it hit the cold air. As I took a knee next to him, his blood stained the entire rock face and his body was emptied from the life source. His face was frozen in a surprising emotional manner as if he didn't see his fate coming. His hands were still curled in a praying manner, like he was begging for his God, one last time. I secured the grenade, then checked the surrounding area for booby traps.

Jesus, this is messy. I thought. *Then again, when is it ever not?* I felt bad for him in a way even though he tried to kill us. Each kill we racked up always made me feel a little bit more empty.

Already having had one scare, we did not want the other enemy fighters to regroup and attack us while EOD was trying to disarm the IED. SSG Cas ordered me to lead a small team around the mountain bend where the two enemy fighters had run off to and hunt them down. As we approached what we thought was their location, two AH-64 Apache helicopters arrived on station and were able to utilize their infrared cameras to spot the enemy fighters moving around us. The helicopters fired a few of their hellfire rockets and eliminated the threats for us, thus allowing us to move into the area.

We walked up the mountain to conduct a battle damage assessment (BDA). This is the professional term for, collect up the body parts and check for intelligence. We could not see where the bodies were at, initially, but we could definitely smell them as we found them burnt to a crisp and smacked up against a rock. Standing in a rocky washed out draw, south of the IED digging site, I stared at the enemy bodies that didn't even look human.

I sent one soldier back to the truck to grab body bags and instructed the other soldier to pull security while I searched the bodies. Both of the soldiers with me were younger and this was the closest they had been to the enemy (or a dead body) yet, and I did not want to have to expose them to it all at once. *I remember how much of a toll seeing my first dead body took on me.* The shredded bodies of Taliban fighters were gravely maimed and distorted. The hellfire rockets had burned and seared them to the point that seemed to be in the later stages of rigor mortis.

As I moved body parts around to find their pockets, I searched through whatever they had that could be used for intelligence. *Finger, no. Leg, no. Piece of his left jaw, no. Papers, bingo.* Midway through my search, a cell phone could be heard ringing on the dead body, but I could not find it. Quickly though, I saw the light of the phone illuminating from his open ribcage. His vest pocket had been burned into his skin and the cellphone was stuck in between his lung cavity and chest wall. *Well, this is disgusting.* I immediately ended the call, but the same phone number kept trying to call over and over again. I started to catastrophize the situation in my head.

What if the number that is ringing is from the other enemy fighters? What if this guy does not answer his phone and they send more enemy fighters to this location? I only have two soldiers and myself, completely exposed, and we are not in the best position to engage in a gunfight.

I took a picture of the phone number and secured it in my pocket with the hope battalion could trace the call and find usable information from the person on the other end. Grabbing and rolling body parts of the enemy fighters into the body bags I hurried my soldiers to drag them down the hill and mount back up into the trucks. Then, I heard a loud crack as if someone had snapped a branch in half. I looked back to see one of the soldiers pointing his flashlight at the body bag where the head of the enemy fighter had gotten stuck in between two rocks snapping his neck in half. While attempting to evacuate one of the two corpses down the hill, the one body kept getting caught on the surrounding terrain. The soldiers were doing their best to maneuver, but rock after rock kept grabbing the corpse. It was like the valley didn't want to let him go. The obstacles and the fatigue of the battle were making the soldiers nearly delirious as they struggled against the environment. While trying to loosen his head from the rocks, I heard someone yelling off to my left. It sounded like SGT Bemis was yelling at someone. I ran over to see SGT Bemis pointing his weapon at a rock pile and an enemy fighter crawl out with an AK-47 in his hands.

This son of a bitch got us a live one and just like that, this guy had come out surrendering and was giving up terrorism. Quitter. I guess he didn't want to end up like his friends that he had just witnessed get the business from us.

We all moved down the hill to process our detainee and conducted forensics on the dead bodies to ensure we did not have any high value targets (HVTs).

"They want us to identify them, Sergeant?" PFC Kite asked.

"Yeah man, just get some pictures of their faces and check their fingerprints," I replied.

"What faces, Sergeant?"

"Look man. Just get what you can. Battalion wants it done, so just do it." I was frustrated and tired. Dragging dead bodies down a mountain and then playing with their body parts like a Mr. Potato Head, was not on my wish list in the early morning. Don't get me wrong, I'm always down to get some kills, but I just wanted some breakfast.

I shouldn't let my emotions get the best of me toward my soldiers, I thought. I felt bad for Kite having to be exposed to such gore. I knew I couldn't always protect the soldiers from the sights of it all. War is war and they signed up for it. I understood that. But I also knew the aftereffects of it all from my first deployment, and he was never going to be the same after playing with these playdough-looking bodies. If I could've taken the brunt force of the emotional and psychological toll for my soldiers, I would have taken every opportunity to do so. I was already too far gone from my first deployment I knew there was no turning back for me, but they could still be saved.

As Kite took pictures of their faces and checked their fingerprints, I looked down into the black Zip-lock sized body bag examining the enemy fighters. Now, there are two people in this world I can recognize almost immediately: my wife and Ryan Reynolds, *hey-oh*, but there was no way any forensics team was going to be able to identify Mr. Burnt Berry that I was looking at. He just looked like a blob of body parts mixed in a bowl of Chili's con queso from their appetizer menu—*delicious, by the way!*

Once we were finished, we put the bodies in the back of our trucks so that they were not just lying on the road for the local children to see at sunrise. We had to wait for the Afghan police to arrive and take the bodies away to perform the proper burials. According to their religion, they have 24 hours to properly bury the bodies after they are cleaned and viewed only by the family. They are then wrapped in a shroud. Once buried, they do not use caskets so that their bodies are one with the earth with their heads facing toward Mecca. Mecca, is an Islamic holy place in Saudi Arabia, the center of the Islamic world, and the birthplace of both the Prophet Muhammad and the religion he founded.

Dragging Burnt Berry to my truck, I walked past SSG Reyes who was hanging out of the 4-foot hole he'd been digging. One hand of his was being pulled by a soldier, his other gripped onto an barrel-sized IED. Once the IED was placed on the road, he snipped a few wires and went about his day. *I told you they were crazy.* I opened the back of my truck where PFC Doyle helped me grab the body bag and slide it in. You could tell he was uneasy having to sit next to the dead body of the enemy fighter he hated. Doyle had so much anger in him, he was cursing at the body bag and clinching onto his pistol as if there was a possibility the enemy fighter would come back to life next to him.

"Doyle, calm the hell down. Do not touch the body and put your pistol away. Act right!" I yelled.

I wasn't mad, but I knew locking him back in that truck with a dead body could take a serious toll on his head. Doyle already had up to thirty kills thus far in the deployment, so he'd had his fair share of people trying to kill him on a daily basis. I wanted to get my point across; just because we'd won that day, didn't mean we couldn't have some respect for the dead.

I couldn't blame him though. I remember how rage filled I was on my first deployment. I was so young immature, and naive to the bigger picture. I asked myself, When did this all become so normal to me? How the hell did I even get here?

Wake up.

Two Knuckles Deep

2008

Los Angeles, California

My name is Sean Tobias Ambriz and I'm originally from Los Angeles, California. More specifically, the Redondo Beach area. I was a quiet child who was raised Catholic and served as an altar boy every Sunday. *Put that on your Tinder.* I have a younger brother and sister, both of whom I love more than anything else even though I haven't always shown it. Growing up, I played Pop Warner football and was an all-star catcher during baseball season. I didn't have many friends except for those I played sports with. During high school, I participated in two years of varsity track and four

1996, working as an interior designer. Note the key Power Ranger curtains.

years of varsity football. Although I was a huge advocate of football and it ran my entire young adult life, I only served as co-captain as a leadership position. I knew my place and role on the team, and being a vocal leader was something that I did not learn until later in life. Even though I was somewhat of a quiet kid in school, I was humbly selected by my peers during my senior year to be recognized as Prom King while my brother was selected as Homecoming King. *Ohhh kill em!*

Redondo Union High School Varsity Captains. Sean pictured in middle, Tony on the far right. 2006

I had a great childhood and I was always taken care of, so no complaints from me. I didn't have any crazy life-altering situations that drove me to the military. I didn't grow up with anger and emotional issues. I really didn't have a burden to carry that would evolve me into a great soldier. Everything I would eventually learn on being a good soldier was through my future leaders. Thankfully, I had supporting family members who helped build my emotionally based foundation. *I was always told being emotional wasn't a bad thing. Emotion just means you care and caring hopefully guides a good leader.*

Brother Tony and Sister Brianna. 2017

My parents divorced when I was young, but I adjusted with it because I got some pretty cool stepparents in return. Most kids don't have a genuine relationship with stepparents, but that was not my case. My mother is Polish, and my dad is Mexican-Native American. I love all of the cultures and heritages I am involved with, but over the years my Native American heritage has naturally appealed to me the most. The Native American warrior spirit is a real and long held traditional spirit that lives in all blood of Native Americans who are able to step into the dark places within themselves. The warrior culture tradition has always been instilled into the youth. My grandmother poured it into me when I was young and drove stories of honor and courage into my heart every day. Whether it was picking me

Sean and his grandmother playing Bingo, 2010

up from school or driving me to practice, she would tell me stories of her experiences, family history, or lessons she learned at the local high school she worked. Every story she told me had meaning and she was never one to back down from anyone. When she was younger, my grandma was a black belt in karate and always stood up for what she believed in—even though she only stood at a meager 4'11". She also loved hitting my brother and I when we made smartass comments. A quick swift punch to the kidneys was always her favorite with, each strike made out of love. She always made sure that her grandchildren understood what honor, tradition, and a warrior spirit meant. I think any Native American that serves his or her country has a goal to serve because of our sacred purpose to protect the land and water of our country, which are the soul givers of life.

Fun fact: there used to be an Army Regulation (AR 70-28) that regulated procedures for Army aviation aircraft names. Some of the helicopters that the Army has had in its arsenal over the years are the Apache, Blackhawk, Kiowa, Lakota, and Comanche. There was a mutual agreement between the United States Army and Native

American tribes that created an approved list of names for aviation equipment. They were chosen and approved by the Native American tribes as they needed to promote confidence and an aggressive spirit in the helicopters. After the names were approved by multiple echelons

Sean and Tony, 2010

throughout the tribe and government, a ceremony was held where the tribe leaders conducted a ritual on the aircraft during a blessing ceremony before it went into service.

Okay, sorry I got sidetracked.

Throughout my time in school, I was an average student who maintained some hardcore C's and placed little interest in life after school. Graduating from high school felt like a huge achievement and I couldn't have been happier. *I was an adult now, right?* I got to sleep in, go to the gym, and hang out with my brother, a past time that very quickly came to an end.

My brother Tony, who was my best friend growing up, sort of got adopted into my family. We wanted to keep him away from Inglewood, a suburban area known for gang activity and drugs in

Sean and Tony, 2019

south Los Angeles. He came over one day and just never left. As much as I loved it back then, having my friend with me all the time, I'm even more grateful now that my mom didn't even question his presence in our home. She was more welcoming than anyone could ever have been. She fed him, put clothes on his back and ensured the roof always stayed above his head. Still to this day, we take family pictures as if he has always been one of her own children.

The best thing I ever learned about Tony was that he never used the situation he came from to his advantage. He never brought up

being from a poor neighborhood and he never used it as an excuse to get what he wanted. He is one of the most mentally strong people who never took "no" for an answer, and he always had a solution to a problem.

Sean and Tony, High School Graduation, 2007.

Not long after high school, I watched as he applied for dozens of scholarships as well as applying to the number one college of his choice: the University of Michigan as a means to go back to the state he was born in. I was super proud of him and it's not like I had a doubt in my mind that he wouldn't make it, but in my head, we were just going to keep doing this sleeping in and gym thing until we got old. Making money and having a career path just wasn't my priority. *My mom will just support me my whole life, right?* What a idiot I was. Before I knew it, I watched as Tony packed up his things and headed out to Michigan with a full ride on the Bill Gates Millennium scholarship that he had received for being one of the top 300 students of the year and placing in the top ten percent of his graduating class across the entire United States.

So yeah, he was super smart. Way smarter than I'll ever be.

As I was left home alone, I watched my peers along with Tony continue their education and careers outside of Los Angeles while I kept waking up and doing the same thing completely lost and not knowing which route would be the best for me. *Hey Alex, can I get*

First Adulthood Depression for 200? I would webcam Tony every couple of days to keep in contact with him, but we both saw a difference in my demeanor. I was letting my peach fuzz facial hair grow out, as well as letting myself go physically. He could tell I wasn't happy, and I was depressed being at home alone while everyone else was going out and making a difference with their lives. Tony had even walked onto the football team and got to fulfill his dream of playing as a Michigan Wolverine. He even won a Rose Bowl ring with them.

Ok, I have to do something!

I decided to aim pretty high I signing up for two classes at El Camino Community College. *Yeah, watch out ladies.* I spent one semester going to two classes. I couldn't even tell you which classes they were as I only went half the time. I also played one season of football earning a conference ring, but it still was not as fun as high school. I quickly realized that the classroom just wasn't for me. I needed something bigger.

Tony playing football for the University of Michigan

A very key moment in my life was when I made the decision to join the military through a very immature decision over my high school sweetheart. I had been dating my girlfriend Denise for over two years, but she was a year ahead of me and already in college. As I was dragging my feet toward finding a real career, she was working toward a future in the medical field. She was a hell of a lot more mature than I was and tired of seeing me be so lazy wasting my life away after high school. I remember her asking me what my five-year plan was. In reality, I didn't even have a five-day plan. So, what did my logical thinking eighteen-year-old self-come up with? I'm pretty sure the military is handing out five-year plans!

Military? Could I handle it? I'd be jumping into a war time army. This war wasn't even a concept to me when the United States was thrown into it on September 11, 2001. I was woken up early that morning by my dad. Watching the news, I didn't understand what it all meant. I thought it was an accident. I had no idea I would one day be walking into a piece of history handed down to me.

Growing up, I used to play soldier in my grandma's backyard with my cousins. From head to toe, we had the latest and greatest gear and highest technologically advanced weapons "Pick N' Save" could buy. I had always enjoyed watching videos of Marines in Fallujah and a part of me subconsciously wanted to serve my country in some capacity. So, I went down to the local Marine Corps recruiting station and tried to figure out what options would best fit me. The marine recruiter I talked to was very blunt and had little time to deal with my indecisiveness. He was very aggressive in his approach, calling me every morning for two weeks straight at 6 a.m. to let me know that I was being a huge bitch for taking my time in joining. Don't get me wrong, as much as I loved being called a bitch, I wanted to make sure that I was stepping into the right career field, so I decided to maybe try out the Army instead.

The Army recruiter told me that he was a cook, *so you know he was a badass.* While he wasn't the picture-perfect soldier you saw on TV, he was a genuine person who told me what was best for me and not just what I wanted to hear. I wanted to be a Ranger, but at the same time I wanted a job easily transferable back into the civilian sector when I got out. He persuaded me into looking into the Military Police Corps, Which has a little bit of handcuffs and little bit of explosives. I couldn't argue with that. The plan was to do five years on active duty and then return to Los Angeles to pick up a job with LAPD. Little did I know, the brothers that I found in the Army, coupled with our time spent in Afghanistan, would completely change my plans—*thanks a lot, Bin Laden.*

Even though my career would not pan out to be too much police work, I still do not regret how it turned out. The Military

Police Corps would give me more than any other branch or service department ever could have.

My parents wanted me to continue college and then enter the military as an officer. Earning more money with higher levels of responsibility was the bigger picture they were painting. With the war at its peak, I just wanted to be in the grind with the enlisted. *I am not saying going officer is a bad route, it just wasn't for me.*

My first step into the military was in 2008 at the Los Angeles Military Entrance Processing Station (MEPS) when I chose to accept the Military Police Corps. *What an experience that place was.* I have gone almost twelve years now asking random soldiers of their experiences at their individual MEPS buildings and mine seemed to differ from each one of theirs. I remember how nervous I was when my recruiter drove me there that day, escorting me from room to room, and signing papers I had no idea what they said. For making such a huge adult decision, I was too young and stupid to realize half the things that were going on around me. I'd taken a leap of faith and jumped into a career field I had no idea about. Moving from station to station throughout the building, each floor containing the next series of instructional in processing stations. Majority of it was administrative paperwork and contractional signing, until you got to the creepy medical examination room that looked like they were going to manipulate you into the human centipede, asking a bunch of eighteen year old males to strip down into our boxers and duckwalk across the room.

After the awkward half-naked duck walking contest ended, then came the individual medical physical. Now, like I said I've asked a lot of people in my time how their MEPS experience was and theirs seems to be a little off than what I had to go through. When I was invited into the examination room, an elderly male doctor asked me to remove my clothes so he could conduct a physical. I had done plenty of these growing up playing football each year, and it really wasn't a big deal to me—pull your pants down, put your head to the left, place ball sack into doctors' hands, and give a good deep cough. *Too easy.* When I started to put my clothes back on after having been examined, however, the doctor asked me to face the table and bend at the waist. *I'm sorry, what?* The doctor put one hand on my lower back and the other with a latex glove went two knuckles deep into my you-know-what.

"Hmm, you seem to have some blockage," the doctor said.

"Ugh, then take your finger out sir," I replied.

After my first real date in the military with this doctor, I sat back down in the hallway next to another candidate who was inprocessing and had finished his examination before me.

"Man, that whole finger in the butt thing was kind of weird right?" I asked the other male.

"The what? What are you talking about?" he asked.

"The . . . the finger, with the glove and the . . . butt?" I stuttered.

"Yeah, no one had a finger anywhere near my butt," he said.

For the remainder of the day as I was in processing, I took every chance I got to ask every other individual male if they had received the same affectionate attention from the doctor I had, which 100 percent of them denied ever happening. To this day, I wonder if that guy was really even a doctor.

Oh well, you have to laugh at the situation. I am pretty sure I can't be the only one who got the five-star treatment. Most guys are probably just too embarrassed to talk about it. Little did I know, that was the first day the Army would provide me with such treatment.

After I signed the contract and raised my right hand, I officially started my journey to become a soldier. I had my chest out and my head held high. I was motivated. You couldn't say anything in that moment to bring me down. That was, until I got a text message from my girlfriend Denise saying that she was leaving me. Boy was I devastated. I'd just made what felt like a lifelong commitment and dedicated the next five years of my life to a career field that I wasn't sure if I was going to be good at or even like—all for a girl. *Fellas, listen and learn.*

As much as it tore me down, because I thought I loved her, it was one of the best (if not the best) immature decisions I have ever made in my life to join. The decision to join for her may have been reckless and spontaneous, but her pushing me to better myself set me on track for the career and life that I have with my family now. So, I can't be mad at Denise one bit. If anything, I owe her my gratitude for pushing me in the right direction.

It was nice to see that I was making my family proud, doing something that was bigger than myself. My grandfather served in Korea, but other than that, my family never served in the military. My uncle, who was on the Redlands SWAT team, was also a helicopter pilot for them as well. My cousin would eventually end up being a firefighter and constantly risk his life in some of the deadliest California wildfires. So, I guess it was in our blood to be warriors putting others before ourselves, but most of the males in the Ambriz family were quiet individuals and, in the military, a quiet professional is a humbled soldier.

After I enlisted, I was shipped off to Fort Leonard Wood, Missouri, for Basic Combat Training with follow on Advanced Individual Training to develop the skills necessary to be a military police officer. After our first three weeks, the drill sergeants were tasked with operating a new program built for a possible surge in Afghanistan. This program was named AMPS, short for Advanced Military Police System. Essentially, it force-fed twelve lucky soldiers along with one drill sergeant through basic training and advanced training faster so we could be shipped to their units sooner for follow-on deployments. Luckily for me, decisions of career advancement were not based on leadership potential, but on physical fitness scores, which boosted me into the AMPS program and out of basic training a month sooner than my peers. My basic training program panned out to be very different from that of the majority and the showmanship of constant yelling and drawn-out hours of physical fitness were cut short so that I could receive the mandatory training required to graduate. Now, I can't tell you if the statistics show that this was a more successful way to get us through basic training, but I do know it was very successful in pushing us through the system and getting us to our units faster so that they could do more in-depth training in preparation for the war.

Graduation Day. One Station Unit Training at Fort Leonard Wood, Missouri, 2008.

3 The Mountain Post
2008 – 2009
Fort Carson, Colorado

Three weeks after basic training graduation and just before the fourth of July 2008, I arrived at Fort Carson, Colorado "The Mountain Post." I was assigned to the 759th Military Police Battalion. *Fun fact: this battalion held the last Mounted Horse Platoon in 1950.* I had never been outside of California, except for a few small trips growing up, so this was a big step for me. My unknowing young mind was not aware that there were mountains in Colorado, nor that with mountains comes elevation, and with elevation comes thin air, which in turn means lower oxygen levels for breathing. My physical state was put to the test, and I quickly realized that I was not quite on the level I had expected myself to be or that I needed to be. There weren't any room for shortcomings when it came to my physical fitness. It wasn't an option. I felt weak, and weak was not something I could be around the group of individuals I was about to connect with.

You know those moments in life when you look back and wonder *what if* this would've happened and how different my life would've been? My first military *what if* moment came as I stood in the S1 shop (the battalions administrative office) and watched my command sergeant major enter the room with a stern look on his face to give us our new personnel brief.

"Are any of you going to give me problems? Are any of you stupid? That's rhetorical. Look, we do not have time for you to do stupid shit here. Take care of yourselves, take care of the people on this post when you are working, and listen to your leaders! Do you understand?" he demanded.

Thank God he wasn't looking for an answer on that whole stupid set of questions.

The sergeant major pointed straight at my chest, with his fingers extended together in one of the strongest knife hands I had seen. "You," he said looking at me and then swung his arm to the two other soldiers to indicate that we were going to the 984th Military Police Company. The three soldiers to my left ended up going to the 110th Military Police Company.

What a way to decide my fate. We might as well just rock, paper, scissors to decide our unit. Imagine if I stood anywhere else except for where I had been standing in that moment, I probably wouldn't be here. This would always be my first what if moment. Soldiers constantly ask themselves what if wondering if the outcomes would have been different.

When I arrived, my first sergeant placed me into Second Platoon "Punishers", where I was greeted by seasoned Iraq war veterans who had returned with the company a year earlier. These combat-tested NCOs immediately began drilling me with battle drills and weapon systems. My leadership always tried to instill the importance of training on a daily basis. The methodology was to not wait until tomorrow to train, because tomorrow might not come. Deployments will come fast and when they do, you do not want to have to look at your leaders and ask them what to do next. You should always have some level of preparedness in the back of your mind regardless.

I learned a lot from my NCOs and although they were extremely hard on me, I was treated the same as the next soldier. Everyone talks about the old Army. Although I can't claim I was a part of that Battle Dress Uniform (BDU) wearing

Field exercises at Fort Carson, Colorado, 2009.

26

generation, I was definitely raised by them. I see my generation as the last link in the chain between what once was and what is now. Anyone who joined prior to the surge has an obligation and responsibility to carry on what the old Army once stood for while still adapting to the changing culture. Years later, the one thing I always praised my leaders for, was their ability to talk openly about their experiences at war in Iraq. They detailed their stories, not how history books would, but with tales of brotherhood and a group of individuals driving toward a common purpose. I would ask questions about situations they had been placed in, what was effective for them, or what they failed at. I knew that when my time came, wherever the army would send me, I would apply what they had taught me and react based on the successful decisions they made. Their stories of endearment, struggle, and loss taught me more than any Army regulation or field manual ever could have.

I was always nervous when I went to work never knowing what to expect and always trying not to piss anyone off. As much as I got homesick, surprisingly, I was happy with the change and adapted easily to my new life and environment. There was only one bad thing with change: always being the cherry in the group. I hated being the freakin new guy (FNG), but I understood everyone had to bear the burden of the title at some point. I was never hazed by today's standards, but there was some fun in my welcome party. Don't get me wrong, I welcomed everything I received because I wanted to earn my place in the brotherhood and the trust that came with it. On of my first weekends at my new unit, I was invited on a platoon camping trip. I was given directions to the "campsite," which took me to the base of Cheyenne mountain, just outside Fort Carson. Per the directions, I followed a dirt trail through an open gate on which there was a sign reading, "Do Not Enter."

"Excuse me, but I'm a private (E-2) in Military Police Corps. Obviously, I know what I'm doing". *If you could see me right now, you'd see me rolling my eyes. Hard.*

I was no more than 100 yards through the gate when two individuals in military gear, looking like Special Forces, stepped out of some vegetation and stopped me.

"Where are you going, kid?" one asked.

"The… camp… with… my platoon… camping trip," I mumbled like a little bitch.

They laughed, informed me I had been pranked, and told me to turn around. At the time, Cheyenne mountain was a US Air Force controlled area with restricted access, so I had absolutely no business being there.

As for the next ten months, my days consisted of continued initiation, excruciating physical fitness during the harsh Colorado winter, and non-stop field exercises. Soldiers today would view what I endured as hazing or unfair physical punishment (smoke sessions), but I welcomed it with open arms. This was what I signed up for—for the rigorous demands of discipline and attention to detail that my leaders demanded of me. All of this would soon keep me alive. Some days I felt singled out or pushed to the edge, but that was because in my civilian life I was never asked to do more or be challenged as much as I was now. Little did I know that I was being pushed, but not for my own individual achievements and growth. I was being pushed so that when the bullets started to fly up and down that two-way range my leaders and peers would be able to depend on me to do my job with a high level of discipline and attention to detail knowing that their lives would be safe in my hands.

I made really good friends during this time, specifically PFC Wood and PFC Valenzuela. We were all on the same playing field in regard to our mental and physical fitness, and so naturally everything we did was a competition. It was so nice having other people around me who had the same goals and aspirations. Overall, the competitiveness in the platoon made us stronger and brought us closer together, which is exactly what we needed for the future that lay ahead.

My weekends were pretty boring as I never drank alcohol and I was always the designated driver. Every weekend was the same. I sat in my barracks room playing PlayStation®. Waiting for the call from my drunken buddies. After herding them into my truck, I had to strategically maneuver through the McDonald's drive thru trying to order 50 pounds of nuggets, while attempting to keep them from hanging out of the windows. It was annoying, but I am glad I was able to take care of them. I never did much and I've always regretted not taking advantage of living in Colorado, mostly in part due to my NCOs threatening my off time saying that if I broke my arm snowboarding, they would break the other one. This is because in the Army, readiness is a huge deal and rightfully so. A soldier needs to be ready at all times. If our unit got the call to deploy and I couldn't go because of my broken arm then I would have just jeopardized the unit leaving my position open for someone else to get pulled into.

In the summer of 2008, my platoon sergeant seized an opportunity that would lead me to become a nationally certified Emergency Medical Technician (EMT), a position that would make me an asset to the platoon.

"Ambriz, do you want to go to EMT school?" my platoon sergeant asked.

"What's that, Sergeant?" I asked.

"I don't know, but they need one and it's a month away from the unit. Do you want it or not?"

"Yes, Sergeant!"

As I reported to the school, I walked into a small classroom with pictures of human body parts, anatomical graphs, and medical equipment scattered about the room. *What the hell did I get myself into? I literally know nothing about the medical world.* For the next month and a half, I worked long hours, studied the entire book, and practiced hands-on exercises that would hopefully save a life one day. We studied fifteen chapters a week with a quiz every day and a test every other day. My weekends consisted of studying and ride-alongs with local emergency rooms and ambulance escorts. Although it was the most rigorous and mentally draining school I had ever endured, it was very rewarding. I never had an interest in the medical field, but I was thankful for the opportunity the Army had given me to expand on my skills as a soldier. Little did I know that I would be applying these untested skills sooner than I could have ever imagined.

We were scheduled to deploy to Iraq in August of 2009, which was always a dream of mine. Thinking about those videos I used to watch online and the stories I heard from my drill sergeants painted a picture of war one could only imagine. *Key word: imagine. Imagining something like war is nothing like experiencing the real thing, as I would soon come to understand.* As conflict in Afghanistan rose, so did the question of where we would actually end up. Speculation came to a halt in February of 2009 as I stood in the motor pool waiting for my commander to pin private first class rank onto my chest. I remember standing there in silence with the entire company of over 160 soldiers watching as my commander walked up slowly. The only thing you could hear was the snow cracking under his boots. My commander who was normally very joyful and outgoing approached us silently and sternly.

"Bring it in Immortals," he commanded as we watched with apprehension.

"I just received word that our orders to Iraq are canceled," he said.

What the hell? I joined to serve and fight . . . and my dreams of serving in Iraq are being taken from me?

A deep breath followed as he paused. "We are deploying to Afghanistan in less than forty days. President Obama has ordered a surge to help push back a main enemy force that is moving into the country."

Everyone stood in shock. Excitement showed as some smiled across the formation to their friends. Others stood silent with fear and scared shitless with the realization of how unprepared they were. The commander gathered the leaders of the company while the soldiers were dismissed to start prepping their gear for field rotations and deployment mobilization. Online training and repetitive briefings seemed to come to a complete halt as rapid equipment fielding became priority numero uno. Finally, I was seeing the Army in the light for which I joined. Tension grew among the leaders as they ensured their soldiers were squared away. Team leaders were meeting with their squad leaders to finish establishing the standard operating procedures for tactics in the case of combat. Studying increased as officers examined the layout of Afghanistan and read history books to learn from the mistakes of our predecessors.

As we prepared for the deployment, our unit took priority over all other units for ranges. The entire company went through multiple ranges, qualifying on all weapon systems and zeroing optics. One of the biggest urban training sites was reserved for us to use in a two-weeklong field cycle. We were not sure if we were going to be fighting in urban terrain in the south or guerrilla style in the mountains to the north. We did training exercises for both situations using the Colorado elevation to our advantage, by conducting urban operations during the day and maneuvering in the mountains at night. When we trained, we were in full kit walking up and down the mountains conditioning our lungs and legs to the terrain we would be fighting in.

One day, during a lunch break, my good friend Justin Riling and I stood looking out over the quiet Colorado mountains trying to imagine what the future held for us.

"Do you think we're going down south to the desert or north in the mountains?" Justin asked.

"I don't know man. I just want to go already. I'm nervous, aren't you?"

"Kind of, but we've got the best platoon, with the most experienced leaders so I'm not too worried about it," Justin said. "Plus, I packed four packs of Marlboro Lights and a case of Mountain Dew, so if I die, I'll at least be happy."

"Shut up Justin, you aren't going to die," I replied.

I chuckled, playing off our dark humor and ignoring the twinge of uneasiness that I felt as I thought about the reality of our possible death, which came with the job. To be honest, I wasn't sure if he was joking or not. One thing I learned and

SPC Ambriz and SPC Riling, 2010.

adapted to as my time in the military went on was the dark sense of humor we all had. In the civilian world, delivering a joke about suicide at any time is considered a red flag and poor decorum. In the military community, however, it marks you as a well-adjusted soldier. The sad part of it is that most of us who have seen combat seem to possess passive aggressive suicidal ideations. Having a dark sense of humor is the way we cope with accepting the risks we take and the possibility of giving our lives for a bigger cause. Flushing out the thought of getting through the deployment alive helps us not to freeze during times when decisions are a matter of life or death.

Once our field training was complete, our company sent us to a weeklong battlefield forensics class that had us utilizing pieces of equipment that could identify individuals on an HVT list by scanning their irises and fingerprints. The class was very formidable and set me up for a lot of success. I learned a lot and on the last day instead of taking a test, the instructor gave us a challenge. Whichever team came back with the highest-ranking individual submitted into their piece of equipment would win a surprise. PFC Mihalsky, my teammate for this assignment, decided we should go balls out and hit up the Fourth Infantry Division commander.

Sounds good to me, what could possibly go wrong?

We carried the piece of equipment in a black briefcase into the division headquarters and reported to the staff duty desk. There was no clearance or badge authorization into the building. We just straight up told the guy at the desk that we needed to see the division commander by showing him our briefcase and giving it a little tap. Looking confused, the young sergeant pointed us upstairs. *I can't believe this is working.* Each flight of stairs brought us to a higher ranking individual—first, a sergeant major, then a lieutenant, followed by a major, and then a lieutenant colonel. Each one of them got the same response from me, a private first class, patting my briefcase and telling them I needed to see the division commander. Finally, on the third floor I waited outside the passcode-enabled door of the division headquarters room. When the first individual came out, I snuck right in. Just outside the division commander's office we ran into a full bird colonel (COL), who stopped us in our tracks. *It is like running into Bowser in Super Mario Brothers!* With no way to convince him as to who we were, why we were in his headquarters, or why we needed to see the division commander, there was no other option but to accept defeat. As we started to walk away, there came the voice of the division commander.

"Who is that? What's going on out there?" Major General (MG) Hammond asked.

"Some privates, sir. They were just leaving," the COL said.

"Bring them in here," he announced.

Once we were standing in front of the general, nerves took over and our plan went out the window. *Okay, yeah this was about as dumb as I thought. Well, we're here, and I'm already going to get in trouble, so let's make it worth it.* I slammed the briefcase onto the division commander's desk and told him that we were there to input his information into this piece of equipment that we were working with for our training exercise.

Completely confused, he agreed and was willing to spare a little time for us soldiers. After we finished inputting his information, we tried to rush out of there before we could get into any more trouble. We thanked him and started to head out, but he stopped us in our tracks.

"Come here you two. You know, in all my years serving as a commander, especially as a general, I've never seen two Privates have the balls to walk into my office and talk to me like you two did."

As we stood there at the position of attention, waiting to get our shit pushed in, we saw his hand extend out toward us with two coins in his palm. Looking up, I saw he was smiling and congratulating us with a coin of excellence. *I could not believe it.*

"By the way, I need to have a talk with my physical security NCO about how you two got in here."

Fun fact: Every commander has his or her own version of a coin, which usually has a representation of the unit motto, insignia, or some form of unit distinction. Coins come in all different shapes, sizes, and colors. The history of the coins in the military vary from story to story. One story is that during the First World War an officer was handing out bronze medallions featuring the insignia on them to the pilots. One young pilot was shot down and taken captive by the Germans, who removed everything he had in his pockets, except for the coin. Eventually, the pilot escaped the prisoner of war camp and fled to France, where he showed the French the coin to prove his identity and he was returned to safety.

As our time at home came to an end, the anticipation of where we were going to end up pulsated in our minds. Standing on the flight line at the Colorado Springs Airport, I looked around at my NCOs with my heart racing in my chest. Leaders like SGT Ring, CPL Powell, CPL Systo, SSG Brown, and SGT Kiel looked nonchalant and confident and completely unphased by what was waiting for us at the end of this plane ride.

"Hurry up, Ambriz!" CPL Powell said spitting out a huge dip.

"Roger Corporal," I smirked.

Corporal Powell was one of the team leaders in my platoon. A heavily experienced combat veteran, who had deployed twice before and was an engineer in Iraq where he had received a Purple Heart. As the result of an RPG taking out one of his nuts. *Literally, he completely lost a testicle.* He was also the point man during his deployment. Going from building to building, he was once shot twelve times entering a room by a teenage kid. All of the bullets were stopped by his vest plates. He was a hard ass, and extremely country, but he was the one person you wanted to run into hell with. I was lucky to have the

SPC Powell receiving his Purple Heart in Iraq.

team leaders that we did in this platoon. The majority of them had combat experience, and those that didn't, you couldn't tell. They were so confident in their jobs, and the ability to lead seemed to come so naturally to them. The only reason I wasn't more nervous was because of the leadership I had around me, which was a source of comfort that ended up sticking with me the entire time we were there.

The days went by and we traveled from Colorado to Maine, Maine to Germany, and then to Kyrgyzstan, where we in-processed, staged, and waited for takeoff to our final destination: Afghanistan. For a week, we stayed on an Air Force base in barracks with mattresses, a 24-hour dining facility, computers, and shopping. *Not too bad for a deployment. I should've joined the air force.* I loved having midnight chow and a never-ending supplied of candy. Come to find out, they supply candy, shopping, and other amenities was because we were going to Afghanistan and it may be our last chance to indulge. *Way to be a mood killer.*

The day finally came to board our plane to Bagram, Afghanistan. My nerves were completely shattered, and any logical thought process that I had was gone. In full kit, bag front-loaded onto my chest, I followed a line of my fellow military policemen up the ramp of the aircraft. I sat in a cramped middle row of a C-17 and watched the light transform from green to red indicating we had crossed over into Afghanistan's air space. No one told me that the C-17 pilots were trained to conduct combat dives and that they would be performing one. Combat landing is a tactical aviation maneuver that pilots perfected during Vietnam. It is essentially a nosedive at a high rate of speed in which the pilot pulls up last second to help avoid enemy fire when landing. I already hated roller coasters, so it was a total surprise to feel my testicles touching my lung cavity.

Once the combat dive to hell was complete and we had landed, everyone was anxious to get off. That was, until we saw our first group of Americans on the ground. As I exited the ramp of the aircraft, I noticed dozens of 101st Airborne soldiers who were waiting to take our seats. They looked tired, old, dirty, and their uniforms were torn.

Damn, are we going to look like that by the end of this?

Two weeks of orientation, in-processing, and training were conducted only to be followed by hours of boredom. We sat around listening to briefs and waiting for our final push into the war torn area. We received briefs covering anything from the rules of engagement to cultural awareness and mine detection.

Finally, the night came and we loaded the busses that took us to two CH-47 Chinooks. Once boarded, I sat next to the crew chief who looked a lot like he'd previously delivered thousands of soldiers to their final resting place.

"Hey Sergeant, do you know where you are taking us?" I asked.

"They didn't tell you where you guys were going?"

"Come on Sergeant, you know they won't tell my private ass anything."

He looked shocked. Nothing could have prepared me for his answer. "Man, where you're going, a bunch of Navy SEALS died a couple years back."

What the hell? Why are they taking a bunch of MP's to a place that SEALS got killed?

I did not know this at the time, but the crew chief was referring to the infamous Operation Red Wing, which took place in the same mountain range we were heading to—for those of you who are not history buffs, this was the same mission depicted in the movie *Lone Survivor*.

The Chinook landed, the ramp dropped, and we walked in a single file off into the darkness. Stepping off the ramp and onto a pile of rocks, I couldn't see anything around me because of the low illumination from the moonlight. Ten feet away from the helicopter, I turned around only to witness my first beautiful image of war: the rotary blades from the helicopters displayed these multicolored lights that shined in a huge circle above us. Most soldiers don't know, but this effect was named after two soldiers who were killed, called the Kopp-Etchells Effect. This physics-producing action displays these beautiful lights that are created from the rotary blades. With the blades spinning as fast as they do, they kick up a lot of dust and dirt, which results in a lot of static electricity created by the friction. When the sand hits the blades, the heat particles around them heat up themselves, and create this beautiful glowing halo.

Standing behind the engines, hot air blew in our faces as we unloaded our bags as fast as we could while the crew chief yelled for us to hurry. In a place like Afghanistan where you are surrounded by the high ground, the enemy can always see down onto you. Having a helicopter or any large piece of equipment sitting in the same spot for too long allowed the enemy to dial in on it, destroy it and score a psychological victory. Within a minute, the platoon was unloaded, and the helicopters had ascended above us and over the mountain range. My eyes were open as wide as possible trying to see any movement in front of me, but all I could see were dark shadows moving around. The sound of the helicopter faded into the distance and voices around me increased, trying to get a sense of where we were. A monotone-voiced individual trying to get our attention rang out from above the flight line.

"Welcome to FOB Blessing. I need to get all of you out of the open. Follow the chemlights on the ground to your rooms. We will have follow-on instructions for you in the morning. Welcome to the Stan."

So this is how I'm introduced to war? I get kicked off the back of a helicopter into the darkness not knowing where I'm at or who I'm following, and trusting some chemlights are going to lead me to where I need to be. The only emotion I have at this point is the fear of not knowing what's next. My other emotions can't form themselves yet because I have nothing to base them off of or even see what I could be scared of.

We followed the chemlights up a hill and to our rooms while tripping on rocks and rugged terrain and constantly dropping our bags along the way. The two rooms were empty, except for the eight makeshift wooden bunk beds that were doubled up with two persons per mattress, cuddling to keep warm. After a few hours of sleep, we opened the doors at first daylight to get a look at our new home for the first time. As soon as the door opened, an A-10 jet aircraft flew overhead, which released multiple flares, and conducted a show of force to the east for a unit that was in contact. Our eyes adjusted to the bright light while focusing on the sights of the treacherous mountains that surrounded us. Each side of our base was bordered by the bottom of a mountain face. We were in a fishbowl essentially, completely exposed for everyone to see.

What the hell is this? How are we supposed to fight in these conditions?

The unit we were replacing took no hesitation in introducing us to Afghanistan so they could get out of there as fast as they could. Our first day, they came to us asking for two teams to head out with our leadership and get an idea of the area. I was one of the lucky soldiers to get chosen. It was to be a simple patrol into the local village of Nagalam, "The City of Peace." I call *bullshit*. I remember them opening the gates as we walked out in a column down the road and toward the village. As I locked and loaded my weapon for the first time, I realized that the game of death had been initiated. From that moment forward, I tried watching the replacement troops, but they seemed so nonchalant and after a year of fighting, they couldn't have cared less at this point. I scanned every person, car, vegetation, and building. I was watching people's hands and looking for a certain movement. My senses for sounds increased as I paid attention to multiple high pitch noises that might resemble gunfire. Most civilians went about their day and acted normal, but some saw that we were fresh. They could see our uniforms had never been dirty before and we had that scared look on our faces as we tried to absorb as much information as we could on that first patrol. It didn't take long for the locals to realize they had fresh meat, which meant the Taliban would soon find out they had new target practice.

After a few days of talking with our replacement unit and conducting small walking patrols into the local village, I was pulled aside by my platoon leader, 1LT Nicolson and platoon sergeant SFC Lyle.

"Ambriz, we have to split the platoon up and spread thin to cover multiple police stations," my platoon sergeant said.

"Okay, what does that have to do with me, Sergeant?" I asked.

My platoon leader looked down then back up at me. "We are sending you with second squad to be their medic."

Medic? I didn't know what to say. I was just learning this area and had been training with third squad for over a year, which meant I would be leaving all of my friends.

Am I ready for this job and responsibility?

Nicholson and Lyle were the two main leaders for our platoon and were essentially like mom and dad. Every platoon in the Army is looked at in this sense. The lieutenant (LT) is usually young, straight out of college, and inexperienced; because of this, normally lead in a nurturing way like a mother, and allow dad to do what he needs to do to run the family. The platoon sergeant is of course the dad, who is full of experience and rage. Everyone feared dad and you never wanted to piss him off, but you also definitely didn't want to disappoint mom either. Although in some ways both of my platoon leadership fit those descriptions, they were both also very unique in their own respective ways, which made them beautifully abnormal leaders who were well respected. After receiving the news that I was moving squads, I couldn't help but feel like I wasn't wanted by my platoon. Of course, this wasn't the case, and my platoon leadership was simply making a professional decision. It wasn't anything personal, but I was young, dumb, and in my feelings.

The next morning, I reported to the aid station to receive my brief and a full medical equipment supply. I walked in. Multiple medics sat there looking at me with this strangely vacant stare. You could tell by looking in their eyes that they had seen the unforgettable. The aid station NCO, a tall Staff Sergeant, walked over and handed me an OD green colored aid bag. I looked down at the bag; it was riddled with holes all through the back.

"Here. I'm getting out of the Army when we get back. I don't need this anymore. You can have my aid bag."

"Are these bullet holes in the bag, Sergeant?"

"Yeah, bad day. I wouldn't use this bag if I was you though. Try not to use a bag that looks any different from the others. Use a regular assault pack. The snipers around here tend to go after the medics first, so try to blend in. Good luck kid."

What the actual shit.

Well, I guess this is war.

I understand nobody wants war. It's brutal, but a necessary evil. There are people in this world who are made for this sinister chain of events. There are just some individuals that are crazy for war; they're pumped up by it, and no, they're not mentally insane. They're just genetically programmed for it. Their DNA strands are composed of gunpowder and held together with duct tape. The blood that flows through them is as thick as motor oil. Their skin is plated with old Vietnam flak jackets and they run off of nicotine and adrenaline. These war machines were put on this earth for one reason and you should be glad if they're on your side. The gravity of war pulls them to it. Any chance to jump into the fight and defend their brother, they'll take it. I'm glad I knew such men. These machines were my platoon mates. I still had a lot of learning to do and experience to put under my belt, but those T-shirts would come soon enough. I was not yet ready to be one of these machines, but they were building me up for the job.

2nd Platoon, 984th Military Police Company. Last group lunch prior to deployment, 2009.

Medic
May – September 2009
Kunar Province, Afghanistan

Although I knew there had been ongoing conflict in Afghanistan for decades, I never really had a grasp on the seriousness of its traditional war-torn history. From the moment I stepped off the plane, my immature nineteen-year-old mind figured we were just the good guys trying to make the bad guys go away. Simple, right? I swear I should be a military strategist. However, I would quickly find out that my strategy for war was about as easy as rolling iron dice.

Arriving in Afghanistan at the start of spring was an adjustment to say the least as temperatures were rising above 110 degrees. Not only is spring swamp nut season, but more famously, its fighting season. This was pivotal for the enemy as they used the agricultural changes to their logistical advantage. Spring and summer brought farming and farming brought opium poppy fields. Growing, selling, and exporting these opioids was a way the Taliban funded their fighting. With finances, come jobs, and jobs brought more fighters.

You see, there are three different types of Taliban fighters. The first is the smallest population—but also the deadliest—as they are the extreme idealist who thrive on their desire to end the western movement. The second type holds the majority. They utilize their powerful positions to bully and procure financial gain through the sale of opioids and other illegal activity. The third, a midsized group, are the fighters who are hired by the Taliban to fill the gaps and stand armed with the terrorist organization for a small payment.

Overall though, all three types can go screw themselves.

Afghanistan is divided into thirty-four provinces that serve as the primary administrative divisions. Each province is controlled by a governor that is selected by the president of Afghanistan. The provinces contain multiple districts that are in charge of up to 1,000 different villages. If I were to paint you a picture of the terrain in Afghanistan starting

near the bottom of the country and working my way up, essentially what you would see is steadily inclining terrain. The landscapes in the south are flat, desert regions as opposed to the north where the incline in elevation produces some of the most treacherous mountains on earth.

Specifically, to the north east is Kunar province, which borders Pakistan and is split by the Kunar River. The sharp mountains are carved by the Kunar River that flows 300 miles to the south of the country. Being that these mountains are an extension of the Himalayas, these rugged ranges have very sharp peaks and deep valleys with some of the most complicated barriers and rigorous battlefields. Afghanistan has always been notably rich in mineral resources so its mountain passes have always and will always be of great strategic importance.

2nd Platoon, 984th Military Police Company

The thousands of trails are prime corridors for the insurgents to maneuver in and control much of the territory between Pakistan and Afghanistan. Most of Kunar speaks the Pashtun language, but if you were to drift into valleys—such as the Pech and Korengal or even some of the more remote locations—you would encounter Afghans who speak a rare, unknown language. This language was hard to understand, and the dialect could not be deciphered by our interpreters.

These mountains have held some of the bloodiest battlefields in history and are known for the dark shadows cast by their peaks. The terrains has famously deterred previous foreign invaders from entering their country. The harsh, rigorous mountain terrain, although making for amazing scenery, has rock faces sharp enough to cut deeply through entire armies. Afghanistan has always been known to either build empires or completely destroy them. Great monuments are left in ruins scattered throughout what were the previous battlefields. The signs of war lingered everywhere you went. As you drove along the roads, you could look off the sides down the mountain passes and see burnt out and destroyed Russian tanks left from the previous invasion. Minefields covered 90 percent of the country and Russian weapons were still being utilized, sometimes against us. Elders told stories of the Russians and the horrors they had to endure during the Soviet occupation. It seemed that no one was scared of our weapons no matter how big they were. But, if you ever pulled out a pistol for any reason, you may as well have shown them the hand of God. During the Soviet occupation, Afghans were executed daily by the barrel of a pistol. If you looked close enough, you could even see some of the remains of the Russians manifested in the local children. Some of the Afghan children and teenagers were as Caucasian and red-headed as some of the Americans, which was a clear indication that their mothers and grandmothers had been brutally raped by their oppressors. What was said of the geography itself could be said for the people who lived in it. Geography is destiny and in the eyes of our enemies, their destiny had already been decided for them.

With all of those advantages to the enemy, our platoon was chosen by the commander to have the responsibility of attempting to shape the future of Kunar province. In doing so, we would be stepping into a room reminiscent of hell and would be a part of a small fraction of American soldiers able to call themselves Kunar veterans. If we survived, that is. Having to serve in Kunar was a prestigious honor. Anybody who knows anything about the war in Afghanistan knows that this was the front door to the enemy's home.

For the next year, I would be located in south central Asia in the Hindu Kush—which translates to Hindu Killer—mountains, located near the north eastern border of Afghanistan in the Regional Command (RC) East. Not long after our platoon arrived, strategic level leaders had already planned to spread us thin in order to cover wider areas throughout the mountain ranges. Our platoon consisted of three squads, with each squad containing twelve to sixteen soldiers. First and third squads operated out of FOB Blessing while second squad (the squad I was assigned to) operated out of FOB Bostick. We were told the horror stories about everything that had happened a month prior to our arrival. At observation post (OP) Bari Alai, three US soldiers along with four Latvian soldiers and twelve Afghan soldiers were completely overrun by 200 Taliban fighters. As they seized control of the observation post, one American soldier ended up calling for fire on his own position to try and keep the enemy back. He

received a silver star for his actions.

Little did we know that this was a foreshadowing of just how close the enemy was willing to get to us. As part of one of the main missions of our deployment, each squad was assigned to a number of Afghan police stations and checkpoints throughout the region to work with and mentor. Our sole purpose was to drive to these stations each day, conduct police training, patrols, and conduct weekly key leader engagements (KLE) with village elders in an effort to bring stability and peace to the area. Each KLE meeting seemed to be like the last as another group of Americans came into their village discussing change and their future aspirations for the local Afghan. They looked like they had seen it all and heard more. Each visit was the same as the last. We would show up, place our security, remove our gloves and helmets, shake hands, and proceed to the police station commander's office for a slow and disconnected conversation. We would repeatedly ask for training opportunities with their police force, to review their administrative files, police intelligence, and to conduct joint patrols, but their response was always the same. They painted a picture to us that everything was good and quiet and if we could just give them money, they would be alright.

Dude, we wouldn't be here if everything was good and quiet.

For guys like me, who were experiencing their first combat deployment to one of these wars (Iraq or Afghanistan), were so optimistic about bringing positive change to the Afghans. We wanted to spread our knowledge, lend a helping hand, and contribute as much time as we could, leaving the place better than what it was when it was handed off to us. A part of me saw some change; another part of me saw a waste. When I say a waste, I am not talking about

Village of Nangalam, Pech River Valley, 2009

the overall strategic reasoning as to why we were in the country. I am neither in the position, nor smart enough to discuss those reasons. I am talking about the day-in and day-out knuckle dragging hard work with the one-on-one training alongside the Afghan police. Rarely would you meet a good Afghan police officer who had good intentions and hated the Taliban. For the most part, the officers at our specific stations just wanted to collect a paycheck and abuse their power against people. For instance, throwing rocks at kids to shoo them away. It felt like a bigger waste when we were persistently told more than half the police officers were related to the Taliban. So, as we trained them in the day, they had dinner with the enemy at night. Most of the time they would tell us when they were related to the Taliban or if they had a cousin who was a lieutenant with the terrorist group. You could usually tell just by looking at the police officers who was good and who had bad intentions. The majority of the time you were running off of gut feelings and those spidey senses. When you looked around, you could see which police officers wanted to try to manipulate you and which local children were inching closer to the trucks trying to sketch them out and find weak points for the Taliban.

I'm not saying there wasn't any good change. I did see a vast improvement as time went on and it was equally refreshing seeing a police officer take pride in his job. There were a few police officers who really valued the future of their country. They respected the American fighting force and wanted to learn as much as possible from us. It's just sad that the majority of the negativity in the country always casted a shadow over the positive moments from the war.

Standing watch outside the police station always heightened my anxiety to new levels. With sweat constantly dripping off my forehead, down my cheeks, and into my soaked chin strap, I always struggled to ever see anything through my foggy, condensation-filled eye protection. I nervously scanned every person and vehicle that entered my visual circle. For the first two months, I was on constant edge and my brain ran off relentless anxiety. I didn't trust anyone unless they

PFC Sherbino in FOB Bostick motor pool, 2009

were wearing an American flag on their shoulder.

Every mission brought experience and experience brought a brotherhood. Since I switched squads at the beginning of the deployment, I thought that I wouldn't enjoy myself since I was leaving my friends in third squad. I was wrong. I could not have been put in a better team with two individuals, who to this day mean the world to me. My gunner was PFC Sherbino, a young kid from Michigan who had the best sense of humor of anyone I'd ever met in the military. It was hard to ever get this guy in a serious moment because he was always making me laugh. I never thought I would find myself in a friendship like the one I had with him. My team leader, SGT Kiel, who was from Wyoming and was not much older than us, was a battle-tested NCO who previously deployed to Egypt, Iraq, and twice to Afghanistan.

All three of us had completely different backgrounds and personalities, but somehow we found a connection. Our team was called the Ugly Ducklings and it was plastered in the spray paint across the back of our truck. Our motto was, "Quack Quack Mother (insert explicit word)." I would've given anything for either of them as they meant the world to me and they were all I had at that time.

SGT Kiel, training Afghan National Police, 2009

Our squad grew close fairly quickly, rarely dropping our discipline along the way. When there were shortcomings and lack of discipline, our team leaders were not hesitant to apply pressure.

Let's just say it would be the last time we tried something like this.

After every mission it was our job to refuel the truck and reset everything so that, in case of an emergency or quick reaction, we could just jump in the truck and go. This battle rhythm was interrupted one day when Sherbino and I became lazy and tried to beat the system by just parking the truck so that we could hurry up, go play games, and relax. We theorized that we could just wake up early the following day, refuel the truck before mission, and nobody would know any better. The plan was working pretty well until SGT Kiel decided to spot check his vehicle and noticed that nothing had been replenished for the next day. God help our sweet supple, assholes. Since we had lied to him about the truck, he told us our punishment would be to report to the mayor cell for additional tasks for the next three days. The mayor cell essentially was responsible for ensuring that the base was up and running so that soldiers could concentrate on the mission and not the necessary base maintenance. We were instructed to dig a 6-x-6-inch hole from one side of the base to the other, so that they could install new latrines (bathrooms). It seemed that the punishment was fitting of the crime, so we were willing to accept our fate. It was very physically demanding. For the next three days after running mission, we had to dig over 300 meters of pipeline trench and then mark it with chemlights and tape at night to ensure that nobody tripped in it.

"Looks good." SGT Kiel stood above us, arms crossed.

"Thank you, Sergeant. We're glad to support the freedoms of bowel movements," I said jokingly.

"Okay, fill it up," SGT Kiel ordered.

"I'm sorry?" I asked.

"There's no new latrines, you idiot."

"But, you... you lied to us." I whined.

"You lied to me about the truck."

Oh, touché Sergeant. You got us good. I swore I would never lie to that man again.

Before deployment, when my platoon sergeant sent me to EMT school, I never thought I would actually be performing daily life-saving measures. However, it turned out that I was the driver of truck three in addition to performing duties as a medic on every mission. When I was not on mission, I would perform medical duties in the aid station with the 759th Forward Surgical Team and 3/61 Cav, Fourth Infantry Division medics.

I'm not going to lie, it was a little rough at first, having to do normal military police duties as a driver. I was consistently trying to find new ways to keep our truck up and running, as well as improving some upgrades to manipulate ammunition storage, and faster ways to communicate throughout the trucks. I always felt completely exhausted coming off of mission as it was just the beginning. Work never stopped. I immediately put my scrubs on and went into the aid station to help out with whatever casualties we would get. We were a Role 2 aid station, which meant that the majority of the casualties in the north eastern part of the country would come to us where we would package them up and send them to Bagram Airfield. When we were not actually performing lifesaving measures, we had to practice them. Any chance we got, we were opening books and studying the

latest medical procedures to ensure that we were up to date with our equipment and medicine.

Most of my days consisted of the same thing and became repetitive. Unless our schedule

PFC Ambriz in the Aid Station ,FOB Bostick, 2009.

51

was flipped for night operations or a special mission it consisted of the same thing every day: wake up, breakfast, equipment and vehicle check, conduct mission, aid station shifts, medical study groups, dinner, late night porn session with the boys, and then off to bed. Repeat.

By my fifth month, I had worked on a total of 113 casualties. I kept a tracker in my little green book of each person I had worked on. Of the 113 casualties I'd worked on, 21 died under my care. One thing I learned was that every death, whether there was anything you could have done or not, was yours to keep and live with forever. Even though this wasn't a job that I had asked for, it was one I was blessed with having and that my leaders trusted me to do. It obviously took a huge toll on my mind knowing that there were twenty-one lives lost because of me. It ate at me straight at my core, but time was too valuable to spend it thinking about it. *Bury it. Do whatever you need to do and process it later.* This is what I told myself on a daily basis. Problem was, when you bury it, it becomes a seed. If you let that seed grow, it becomes something far too big to deal with. I also understood that more lives required my assistance and attention to detail, which meant I didn't have time to think about the emotional toll of it all. I can't say I didn't think about it, because it definitely ate at me at night and I often found myself sneaking out to my truck so I could cry alone in the back. One thing I learned as a medic was that if you showed emotion, especially fearful emotion to your casualties, that could be the last thing they saw.

PFC Sherbino and PFC Ambriz on a dismounted patrol, 2009.

It wasn't just the physical treatment of casualties but the psychological sustainment as well that I try to work on. PFC Sherbino and I used to collect pictures of model women out of magazines and paste them throughout the back of the truck. When you opened the back door of our truck you were greeted by a plethora of beautiful bikini clad women to look at while you sat in the back. Now, there was a method to the madness. If I were to take a casualty into the back of my truck, as I worked on them, I would talk to the casualty (if they were conscious) about the women that were hanging up in the back of the truck. I would tell the casualty

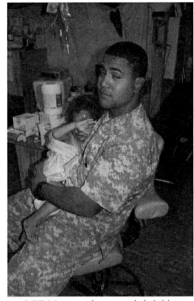

SGT Moore with a wounded child in the aid station, 2009.

that I knew all of these women back from Los Angeles. I'd have them pick one out and tell me what they liked about her. I would make up a story about her name, where she came from, and I would tell the soldier that if he stayed with me I'd hook him up with a date when we got back home. This would keep the wounded entertained, put their mind at ease, and distract them from the pain. Sometimes it even lowered their blood pressure, keeping them still enough that I could work on their wounds.

I enjoyed being a medic, or "doc" to others. I enjoyed taking care of soldiers and bringing a little bit of healing to their daily suffering. Being a medic was like having infant babies-Rage-filled, killing, drunken babies who made things go boom. It wasn't always fun during sick call—sticking my finger in someone's ass to check their temperature, wrapping sprained ankles, or prescribing 800mg of ibuprofen for any injury known to man. But, it was my job to ensure soldiers were mentally and physically capable enough to skull drag the enemies of the United States on a daily basis.

I saw more than I could have imagined being a medic. I witnessed the best and worst of people. Some sacrificed themselves for the betterment of another human being while at the same time watching others inflict pain on another for no reason. My very first casualty was an elderly man who bleeding throughout his upper torso and was dropped off at the front gate. SGT Moore (my medic NCO partner) and I drove the Gator utility vehicle to the front gate. SGT Moore drove while I placed the man in the back and started to work on him on our way back to the aid station. I saw he had been shot in the stomach so I nervously placed combat gauze inside while applying pressure. I could see he was having trouble breathing and was reaching to me as if he wanted to tell me something.

What does he want? Oh shit, the exit wound! What a rookie mistake. Come on Ambriz, focus. Find the exit wound, run through the steps.

With my right hand on his stomach applying pressure, I rolled the man to his right as I used my left hand to feel around his back for an exit wound. As I traced my hand from his lower back, five inches up my hand disappeared and went inside his torso into a hole the size of a baseball. We both looked at each other and as I apologized, the old man smiled and gave me a thumbs up as he started to regain his breath.

Although 60 percent of the casualties I worked on were civilians, nothing could prepare me for actually working on a wounded American soldier. Having someone else's son or daughter's life in my

PFC Ambriz and SGT Moore, FOB Bostick, 2009

hands was particularly gut wrenching. My very first American casualty was one that I would never forget due to my mistakes and poor judgment. Usually when we received the casualty, we all had a set job to do that we would rotate whether that be managing blood, IV, finding additional wounds, checking blood pressure, X-ray, etc. Well, I was in charge of the IV that day and when he was placed at our bedside, I almost lost focus seeing another American in so much pain. As I

Medics cleaning blood off a canvas litter, FOB Bostick, 2009

struggled to grasp the eighteen-gauge needle in my right hand, while my left hand attempted to suppress his hands from grabbing my uniform for pain relief, his blood was oozing through the stretcher and onto the floor. The lights hanging above my head on the tent swayed back and forth from the wind making it difficult to see the placement of my needle. My latex gloves were filling up with sweat. I tried maneuvering the soldier's hands away for just a second so I could get a good stick into his arm while at the same time trying to reassure him that everything was going to be okay. He just wanted someone to hold, but it was making my job a lot more difficult and shakier. After I had inserted the catheter into his arm, I began running fluids through his body to replenish the blood that he had lost. As a few minutes went by we noticed he was losing consciousness and needed the crash table, which had all of our emergency instruments like the automated external defibrillator to restart his heart rhythm. After ten minutes, he was flatlined and pronounced dead. Upon further examination of his body, we noticed the catheter in his arm had moved and he was no longer receiving the fluids that he needed to replenish the blood that he had been losing.

Holy shit. Did I do this?

Was I not paying attention when he was grabbing me? Did I not get a clean pathway into his veins?

This has to be my fault. I was in charge of the fluids. There's no one else to blame but me. Right?

SGT Moore immediately put his hand on my shoulder and told me it wasn't my fault, and there was nothing more that could've been done since he had already lost too much blood. Accidents happen and I was not the source of the problem. At least that's what he said to make me feel better, but in my mind, I knew this was going to eat at me for a long time. I think SGT Moore thought the same thing, which was why he tried to keep me in the game because he knew this wasn't going to be the last American casualty I was going to see. Instead of soaking in my own pity, the next day we received another American casualty, which he threw at me. His thought process was to think about it, mourn, and move on. He didn't want me thinking that I could not work on an American casualty without messing it up and threw me right back into the fire. I was able to sustain his wounds and package him up for his next flight to the hospital where he would make a speedy recovery. Although SGT Moore pretty much gave me a heart attack, I respected him for pushing my boundaries and allowing me to boost my confidence again.

Moments with casualties were not always glorious and lifesaving. We once had a man bring us an infant child who had burns from boiling water all over her legs from a proclaimed accident. After evaluation and distribution of pain medication for the baby's burns, the man and baby returned days later. This time the baby had burns on her other leg that looked the same as the previous injuries. We had an Afghan interpreter that worked in the aid station with us for incidents like this with local national civilians. After further investigation, the interpreter warned us that he overheard the man that brought the child in was taking medications for himself. He was using them to get high and figured he could come back for more medication if the baby was injured. We notified the Afghan police so that they could handle the situation and drive the justice system themselves. I never saw that man and baby again though.

Children were a huge percentage of the casualties in the area that we served. This was in part due to the Taliban's manipulation of them, the constant firefights, and also previous war manifestations. When the Russians fought in

PFC Ambriz tends to casualty 2009.

Afghanistan in the late 1970s, a lot of landmine emplacements found themselves scattered throughout the country making it one of the most heavily mined places in the world. Seeing kids wounded and mangled was not something I was necessarily prepared for initially, but as time went on, so did my numbness of these events. Although it became a daily routine, it didn't get any easier hearing the blood-curdling cries of babies and children praying to Allah begging for their young lives and looking at me to treat them.

As I stood at a checkpoint one day, I looked at the mountains, listening to the river flow beneath my feet in complete peace with life when it was interrupted by the sound of crying.

"HELP! American! Please," someone yelled from behind me.

I turned around to see an elderly man running up to me with a bulky blanket covered in blood. I couldn't see what was underneath, but I knew exactly what it was. I slammed my medical bag on the ground and took a knee as the man simultaneously placed the blanket on the ground before me. As I opened the blanket, I saw a barely conscious twelve-year-old boy looking up at me and reaching at me with his left hand, which had been blown into pieces. The bones of his fingers were completely exposed and barley intact. The skin of his hand was peeled down the middle and folded over his wrist like an open flower bouquet. I asked the interpreter to explain what happened while I placed a tourniquet above his wrist and folded his skin back on his hand along with wrapping it in gauze to prevent further damage and ensure sanitation.

The interpreter told me that the kid picked up a Russian landmine that looked like a toy and detonated it. We weren't far from FOB Blessing, who were able to get eyes on us from the Tactical Operations Center (TOC) and they watched the events of this encounter unfold in real time.

"Any Punisher element (callsign for my platoon), this is Lethal Main (FOB Blessing's call sign). We see your soldiers working on that patient. Did we cause them to be wounded, over"? The radio from one of my NCOs standing over me could be heard as FOB Blessing was trying to gather more information.

"Negative, an elderly man brought us this child who accidentally picked up a mine. The casualty is packaged up and they are going to head out to the nearest hospital," my NCO responded.

"Roger, remove whatever medical equipment you have placed and point them in the direction of the nearest hospital. New medical rules of engagement. If we did not cause it, we do not treat it," they replied.

"What the hell? Sergeant, I am not removing this tourniquet. The nearest hospital is in Asadabad 19 miles away. This kid would bleed out." Looking up at my NCO, no one moved, all unsure as to which decision to make. The radio was still ecstatic as the TOC kept persisting, and we sent them an update. I looked over at my interpreter and stood up, pointing in the direction of Asadabad.

"Screw this. Tell the man to wrap his grandson back up, keep him warm and from going into shock, and get him to the hospital." I made the choice to leave a tourniquet on and hope for the best.

As I watched the man get into a car and drive toward Asadabad, we heard what sounded like the command sergeant major on the radio yelling for us to return to base for disobeying a direct order.

Well, shit. There goes my short-lived career. The Taliban couldn't get me, but my command sure will.

As we returned to base, I exited the vehicle hearing the command sergeant major yelling at the top of his lungs, asking for the person responsible. I hung my head in disappointment and walked toward him until I collided with my platoon sergeant, SFC Lyle, who was a strong, stern but fair NCO who had seen his share of combat with the 101st Airborne. I looked up from my smaller stature and as I stared into his eyes, he gave me a look I will never forget. It wasn't a look of disappointment, but rather a look of protection and sacrifice.

"Ambriz, head to your room. I will talk to the Sergeant Major." he said.

I didn't know what else to say but "Roger" and continued on to my room. As I walked away, I could hear the command sergeant major yelling at SFC Lyle and from what I could gather, he was taking the fall for me. He was not even on mission with us. He was in the TOC and overheard the radio transmission long enough to gather information and understand the decision I had made. Instead of throwing me under the bus to protect his reputation, he didn't even hesitate to take that ass chewing and protect my innocence. To this day, I haven't forgotten what he did for me and I use it as an example for my subordinate leaders to follow.

After seeing what SFC Lyle did for me, there wasn't anything I wouldn't do for my leaders. If they asked for volunteers, I was there. In August 2009 during the prominent presidential elections, volunteers were asked to establish an observation post protecting these voting booth sites.

The Taliban wanted to control who was the next president through fear and corruption, and our job was place ourselves in front of the Afghan people and allow them the right to vote without fear for who they wanted to lead their country. The mission was simple: Infiltrate in the early morning up a mountain draw, establish a defensive fighting position, overwatch a polling site within Sao Village and at all costs prevent, enemy movement into the area.

During the early hours of a mid-August day, CPT Howard (civil affairs officer) 1SG O'Neil (an Infantry first sergeant) tagged along with my MP team leaders, SGT Kiel, SGT Michigan, CPL Systo, SPC Patsky, and myself as we marched up the mountain face a few hundred meters to establish our fighting position. To the north, was FOB Bostick, to the east was our main objective, Saw Village with the polling sites, to the south were continuous treacherous mountain ranges and to the west was a mountain face of 800 meters taller looking down at us.

We spread the eight of us out as far as we would without leaving gaps in between our sectors. We placed SGT Kiel with his sniper rifle overlooking Saw Village, SPC Patsky and SGT Michigan manned the M240 machine gun to the west. CPT Howard overlooked the north, while CPL Systo was placed to the south. 1SG O'Neil and myself were in the center for command and control purposes as well as medical evacuation so I could evenly reach anyone who was wounded. Once positions were set, CPL Systo placed M18 claymores around our entire position in case the enemy snuck up on us throughout the night because of loss of vision due to the terrain.

We were to hold our positions for three days and do whatever we could not to move and give away our exact position to the enemy. If we needed to utilize the latrine we would have to roll over and piss or

shit or hold it. We brought up more ammunition and weapons than food or water, thinking we could get a resupply at some point and figured ammunition and self-defense held priority at that point.

Defensive positions overlooking Sao Valley during presidential elections, 2009.

Day one brought us boredom as I sat back to back with 1SG O'Neil and laid my head against a huge boulder on my right side. We talked every subject there was to stay awake and remain calm during the claustrophobic feeling of not being able to maneuver from our spot. As the day ended, we took a few enemy pop shots over our heads but nothing that seemed to be too close.

"They are probing us," 1SG O'Neil said.

"What do you mean, First Sergeant?" I asked.

"They don't know exactly where we are, they want to engage us and see if we'll move and give our position away."

Day two was the same as day one, long and boring with little contact with the enemy. Near sunset, I looked back as I heard the first sergeant mumble something. As I faced the east overlooking Sao village, I saw a plume of smoke on the opposite mountain with a little red ball flying through the air. Before we could react, a rocket propelled grenade (RPG) slammed 10 feet from us but luckily, we were protected from the shrapnel by the boulder to our right.

PFC Ambriz during the presidential elections.

Day three brought us tension as elections were underway. Across the mountainside was an infantry unit in contact with the enemy all morning. There was nothing we could do but sit there and watch. Around the afternoon, the enemy was tired of trying to probe for our location and planned to impact our entire area and flush us out. A loud whistle was heard and before we could react, a massive rocket slammed

PFC Ambriz during the presidential elections. Moments before rocket bombardment

into the mountainside 35 meters to the north of our position. First sergeant knew immediately the enemy was going to zero us in with their Russian made B-10 rocket, which was essentially a recoilless rifle that fired a larger rocket straight at you with a higher accuracy.

With a twenty second reload time, the second rocket slammed into the mountain this time 25 meters from our location. When CPT Howard was on the radio, trying to pinpoint the rockets location a third rocket exploded 15 meters away. I looked to the north about 25 meters away holding my breath as I witnessed as the fourth rocket exploded on what looked like our machine gun position.

God no, SGT Michigan and SPC Patsky! I have to get them. I just hope I don't run up on a bunch of body parts.

Disregarding giving our position away, I stood up and ran directly to the machine gun position. I didn't have a choice, I had to ensure they were alive. As I ran up to the defilade position, I saw both SGT Michigan and SPC Patsky face down in the dirt covered by tree branches and debris and not moving. *No please!* I rolled Patsky over and opened his eyes. I saw that he was still alive, but bleeding on his arm and crotch. Just as SGT Michigan sat up, I was waiting for that fifth rocket to land right on top of us.

"SGT Michigan get up, we have to go. Come on Patsky, we have to get you down the mountain," I yelled while grabbing his vest.

SGT Michigan was knocked to the ground and was having a hard time standing up, but he tried to get his bearings straight. I felt useless and alone. I wanted to get them away from the impact area so bad, but I had no help and time was about to run out.

"Please Sergeant, get up, the next rocket is going to hit!"

As the enemy reloaded the next rocket, I waited for the impact. *This is where I accepted my last stand.* Now, I hadn't been the best Catholic over the years and war didn't really help my faith; but to say someone wasn't looking over us at this moment, would be a complete lie.

Just as I pulled Patsky up to move him back down the mountain, I heard CPT Howard scream into his radio, "Bank left, bank left." With Patsky's arm over my shoulder and SGT Michigan at my feet crawling, I looked up to the north. Descending from the clouds were two AH-64 Apache helicopters. As they broke through the cloud cover, the sun shined down onto their blades. They resembled what I could only describe as if they were God's hands coming down to protect us.

They just so happened to be heading back to Jalalabad for a resupply and flew right into our firefight. After hearing CPT Howard jump onto their communication frequency, they did not hesitate to bank their guns to the left, gain positive identification of the rocket position, and execute multiple gun runs before a fifth round could ever land onto our position.

Holy shit! There's no way that just happened.

With my mouth wide open in amazement, I couldn't believe we got saved during the final seconds. I carried Patsky over to a rock and leaned him up against it so I could check his wounds as SGT Michigan finally made his way over and sat down with us. As I stood there, watching the enemy position burn to the ground, I looked at Patsky, who pulled out a cigarette and started giggling.

"Patsky, you're bleeding." I said.

"I know," he inhaled deeply.

"Patsky, your dick is hanging out," I said.

"Would you look at that," he chuckled.

During the rocket bombardment, Patsky tore open his forearm diving for cover and in the process somehow ripped his pant seams wide open and because of the hot weather, he liked to free ball it. I had some extra gauze on me, so I wrapped up his genitals to save his dignity. I then checked on everyone else's well-being while we rode out the rest of the day as the elections went smoothly.

I noticed that during moments like these, combat pushes the neurology to another level. It's hard to explain the thought process, chemical imbalances, and adrenaline that runs through every decision in a matter of seconds. Time in combat seemed to have its own multidimensional timeframe. Everything was forced to slow down around you, although you could react at normal speed. The adrenaline mixed with this multi-dimensional time enabled you to process thousands of things at once allowing you to make multiple decisions. Processing this information also meant that you processed emotions but surprisingly, from my perspective, there was no fear. There just wasn't any time for fear, but that wasn't always the same for everyone. The fear that presented itself to me was deflected because of the training my NCOs put me through, which made everything turn into a fluid motion.

The months went on, and we watched as the enemy adapted to our tactics. The hard part about fighting in the mountains was that you were consistently either in the defense, or sitting below in the open and fighting straight up. We always wanted to fight with the advantage under ideal circumstances, but in Afghanistan ideal circumstances were never in our favor. The enemy always had the advantage with built-in fighting positions and mountainous tunnels for concealment. Half the time it was like fighting ghosts. We never really saw the enemy, except maybe some small movement or muzzle flashes from their weapons. We noticed that, as their tactics adapted, they would conduct high-low attacks on us.

They would attack us from afar, 300 or 400 meters in elevation, from a well concealed position, and with heavy set weapons like anti-aircraft guns or PKMs (Soviet-made machine gun). When we returned fire with our direct fire weapons or called for indirect fire to hit their egress routes, they would purposely get our attention on that one far threat without us seeing the real attack. Simultaneously, a squad-size element would attack us from both sides of the road from near ambush positions, usually 50 meters or less. The Taliban could not compare to our military capabilities and they understood that. They also understood that all warfare was based on deception, which they used to their full advantage, seeing as we played in their backyard.

Our command was taking note to how much contact our platoon was taking as a whole. As a platoon, we seemed to be collectively a shit-magnet. The other platoons in the company refused to believe we were actually seeing this much fighting. Normally, military police didn't see this much nor this type of action. Doctrinally, we were supposed to protect the rear element and were a combat support unit. Over the years in war, MPs became combat enablers and found ways to help dictate how battles were won. My platoon sergeant was sick of outsiders playing the telephone game and talking down on the hard work his soldiers were putting in. Over the course of time, he collected each firefight report, or what we call a Significant Activity Reports (SIGACTS). The all-white binder was three inches thick and stuffed with clear coated page protectors in chronological order. Each page protector was wrapping paper for each SIGACTS report, which was like a daily death present to the platoon. Each report painted a picture of what that day was like for us. Things like the exact location, time, and ammunition status would be displayed. The one thing the reports didn't display, were the close calls and individual near-death events. Some things couldn't be typed in a report, and some days each soldier experienced life-altering events that had no words to enhance the binder anymore.

When the binder was full, SFC Lyle slammed it on the table with the other platoon leaders who were talking behind our backs. The binder was sealed with a cover, a simple punisher skull with the words "The Truth Book," typed underneath. To them, they were just paper filled with events handed down to them. To us who lived through them, they were everything. The truth book was a painful reminder, as its heavy weighted paper carried the memories of our suffering and loss.

I was not sure how I was going to write about some of these events, but I figured that to write about life, you must have first lived it to the extreme.

5 Cut by the Saw

September 2009
Kunar Province, Afghanistan

On September 7, 2009, our squad was parked along Main Supply Route (MSR) California next to the Kunar River. We were conducting an overwatch operation for a mile-long logistical patrol heading north to Forward Operating Base (FOB) Bostick. For three days, we sat in our trucks and were not allowed to exit for any reason due to the high probability of snipers. At one point, we were so bored that we decided to see if we could catch fish in the river—turns out, you cannot catch a fish with a 40mm grenade from a MK-19 machine gun. So, we continued eating our plastic-bagged rations.

Once the convoy passed our location, we followed behind it all the way to FOB Bostick and immediately refit our trucks and went to bed. Normally there was always a unit on Quick Reaction Force (QRF) ready to reinforce any unit in need, but on this particular day they were engaged with another unit, which meant we got awakened about three hours later. Our mission was simple: drive six miles south, pick up a damaged truck, and return it to Bostick to be worked on.

Thirty minutes later, we had the truck hooked up and were ready to return to base. Out of nowhere, our radio went insane as we were told to standby at our location

SPC Ambriz on the roof of the Nangalam Police Station, 2010.

and prepare for a MEDEVAC, which was a medical evacuation for someone who was wounded. We sat at our location in complete silence listening to different radio frequencies to try and gather information for what was going on. CRACK! A loud single shot was heard over head and with the dense incline in terrain it was hard to tell where it came from, although clearly it was a lone sniper. Sitting in an armored vehicle against a sniper was comforting knowing I couldn't be touched; but little did I know, I wouldn't feel so comfortable soon. It was like the enemy was letting it be known they were coming for us.

"Punisher 2-2, proceed to Sao Valley (we called it Saw, as it is pronounced) and meet with Hatchet Platoon for a possible MEDEVAC," FOB Bostick radioed to us. Hatchet Platoon was a cavalry unit that our MP squad was attached too so in a way, we felt very near to them as our own.

As we turned the corner into Saw valley, we saw Hatchet Platoon parked along the edge of the mountain. We were 100 meters from their location, but couldn't get to them as our first truck came face to face with a jingle truck. Jingle trucks were ornament hung sparkled and bedazzled trucks that carried equipment and supplies for both the local populace and coalition forces. The jingle truck's doors were open with no driver or passengers in sight. Our trucks slowly crept toward it not knowing we were driving into the sights of an enemy team to our right up the mountain draw. Once in view, our first gunner spotted an enemy Rocket Propelled Grenade (RPG) raise from behind a rock and he opened fire on the enemy before they could get a shot off. The squad leader ordered the driver of truck one to get out of the kill zone. While attempting to maneuver around it, the driver rammed the front of the jingle truck. As the jingle truck was pushed backward, the wheels turned and the truck was pushed over the cliff edge falling 100 feet; while over fifty 155mm artillery projectiles fell out the back and rolled onto the water of the river.

Well, that's one way to clean out your colon.

As we parked our trucks next to Hatchet, we were confronted by First Sergeant Wallace who immediately started asking for volunteers to go up the mountain and retrieve the wounded.

"We have two squads pinned down and cut off up this mountain draw. We need to hurry up and get them down, who's coming?" first sergeant asked.

SFC Eagan, the Hatchet Platoon Sergeant, and three of my team leaders as well as three cavalry scouts raised their hand, which encouraged me to volunteer and offer my medical services to however many casualties there were.

"Ambriz, where are you going?" 1SG Wallace asked.

"I'm just going to run to the truck and grab my aid bag, First Sergeant."

"No need. They just radioed. They are about 200 meters up. It's going to be a quick snatch and grab. Let's go!"

Little did we know, radio static from the mountain peaks scrambled communication at some point and 200 meters was transmitted when it was actually supposed to be 2000 meters. *Well, shit.*

Starting our incline onto the mountain face, I was the third person behind CPL Systo. Fifty meters off the road, the first bullet landed between Systo and myself from a sniper to the south east across the river and somewhere in the vicinity of Sao Village. I looked in every direction for the sniper. All I saw was rock and vegetation. The sounds of bullets cracking were getting closer and I had absolutely no cover. I used the leaves of my bush to conceal my legs as if they were a sandbag wall. I looked around to my NCOs for guidance.

What are we doing? We don't stand a chance with this disadvantage. We are walking into a lose-lose situation.

With no experience or background of a situation like this, I sat there thinking about the what if scenarios, contemplating with myself that none of this was possible, and that we were not going to make it out of this situation without paying a bigger price; but not by leaders., they took the situation for what it was, analyzed it, and found a way to execute the mission. For the first time, I was seeing true leadership perfectly carried out during the dangers of combat.

"Everyone, get up the mountain, and traverse to the right!" 1SG Wallace yelled.

Under fire, the eight of us stood up and sprinted, in no real formation, in and out of the terrain until we reached the first set of terraced fields. Terraces are platforms cut into the mountainside that resemble steps and utilize rainfall and a built-in irrigation system for farming. We tried to formulate a plan on how to maneuver around the mountain face without being spotted by the sniper, which seemed impossible, by going straight up into a hillside draw. Two Latvian soldiers showed up with their digital camouflage, painted weapons, and amazing man beards. *Yeah, I'm jealous.* They said they heard the chaos on the radio and volunteered to head up the mountain and help their American counterparts.

Picture was taken after the first shot from sniper. Arrow indicates PFC Ambriz.

Kneeling in the terrace cornfield, everything was quiet except the corn stalks smacking one another with the breeze. My lips were cracked, my mouth was dry, and my uniform was soaked from the 800-meter incline spartan race we had just completed. Being so young and not really sustaining any injuries at any point in my life, I thought that all of the training that we had conducted at Fort Carson prior to the deployment would keep me ready for moments like this; but the truth was, there were just some situations you couldn't possibly prepare for—this being one of them. You just couldn't replicate this mountainous terrain in Colorado with being engaged by snipers on both sides, being weighed down by gear physically, and being weighed down by the enemy mentally.

My legs still felt fresh, probably because the adrenaline kept me moving, but my breath kept getting taken from me the higher we went in elevation. I wanted to stop, rest, and get some water so bad. I was almost in a desperate state at that point. As I looked at my leaders, even though they were equally hurting, they kept a straight face and looked ahead toward the next goal. The fact that they weren't even showing signs of quitting kept me moving up the mountain.

I looked over at SFC Eagan who was kneeling next to me and changing channels on his radio to try and gather additional information. We heard there were two US wounded in action (WIA) as well as one Afghan Army WIA with a follow-on American who had been killed in action (KIA).

"We have one Hero, I say again, we have one Hero." Hero was said over and over on the radio, as a term for an American that was killed in action. It's not something you ever wanted to hear and when you did, it made you feel physically sick to your stomach.

"You okay, Sergeant? Who's dead?" I asked.

"My lieutenant." He wore an empty face in his response. He reached down in between his body armor and his chest where he kept a single water bottle filled a quarter of the way. He untwisted the cap and immediately held it out toward me.

"Drink some water, we have to keep you going."

I couldn't believe this. This man was just informed that his partner was killed, more of his men were wounded, we were taking fire from two sides with little to no supplies, and he was willing to give me from his nearly spent water. Blown back by devastating news and his first

1SG Wallace and SFC Eagan scouting for a trail around the sniper positions.

action as a leader was to take care of me and ensure my wellbeing was his first priority. *How does he have that kind of mental fortitude? How does he remain so focused?*

My moment of nurture slowly diminished as the sounds of the corn stalks faded, and the sound of a guitar could be heard playing. I stared up the mountain, in a daze as I thought about Lieutenant Parten. I couldn't believe he was gone. Memories of him in the room, playing his guitar and singing while we sat and talked were replayed in my head. As soon as I heard him sing, it was interrupted and taken from me.

"Hey kid, *wake up.* Let's go. We're going to use the cornfields as concealment. Start climbing with CPL Systo," SFC Eagan said.

I looked to my right and watched CPL Systo start to climb a tree into the next cornfield terrace, I followed suit. As I got to the top of the tree, I threw my weapon over the ledge and started to pull myself up. I came over the edge and was confronted with CPL Systo. His eyes were wide open, and he gave me a sign of silence with his finger over his mouth. He proceeded to turn his radio down and was making minimal movements while laying on his side.

"Shhh, shut up," he said.

"What is it, Corporal?"

"I think we got enemy in front of us."

1SG Wallace pulled his radio close to his mouth and started to inquire with the cut off Hatchet Platoon above us about their location in a whispering manner.

"Hatchet 2, this is Coldblood 7. Do you have any friendly forces in, or near these cornfields?" He whispered into the radio.

"Negative, we are still a few hundred meters above those cornfields. Not us," they responded.

1SG Wallace looked back at us and told us to pull out our hand grenades. We followed his lead, pulled the pin on our grenades, and threw them a short distance in front of our location in the cornfield. After the thunderous explosion silenced and the ringing in our ears ceased, we proceeded forward until we ran into a

LT Tyler E. Parten, a graduate of West Point Military Academy

hole in the ground that led to a small cave and three dead insurgents. As we pushed to the right, we made our final incline on a donkey trail with a rock wall that provided a small amount of cover. I sat crouched behind this wall sitting in donkey shit while Kiowa helicopters were doing repeated rocket gun runs along the mountain to try and find the snipers and we tried to formulate a plan of what to do next. From our donkey path and last piece of cover we had, there was a 200-meter stretch of open ground filled with rough and ridged terrain sprinkled with small vegetation and rock piles. Snipers covered all three angles of our approach. Along the open stretch lay two cut-off squads on both sides of the draw. They were pinned down and unable to move without immediately being shot.

"Pale Horse (the pilots), this is Coldblood 7 (1SG Wallace), can we get to their location without getting messed up?"

"Negative, you're going to have to call in a smoke mission to cover your movement. It is too dangerous," they replied.

Sitting there, I simultaneously watched my leaders analyze the terrain and weigh the odds as rockets flew above our head toward the enemy. *What can I do to help? I feel like I haven't contributed to the cause yet.* I looked out ahead of us and I could see LT Parten's body lying in the open. I couldn't hear the guitar anymore no matter how hard I tried. Instead, I heard the wounded yelling for us to get the LT's body. I snapped out of it. *Wake up!*

"Everyone dump your individual first aid pouches. Give me everything," I announced.

All of the leaders started to dump whatever medical items they had and threw them at my feet. I placed tourniquets in my left cargo pocket, gauzes in my right. I started to triage my medical equipment so that I could easily assess it when I needed to.

"If I go down for any reason, I have all the medical equipment. Take it off my body and help whoever needs it," I said.

As the sunset drew near, we were told to prepare for the incoming white phosphorus artillery rounds, which would provide enough smoke cover in the draw so we could sprint for the wounded and bring them back to the donkey trail.

"GO, GO, GO! Get up and help them." SFC Eagan yelled.

As the artillery smacked into the mountain side and the smoke dispersed, we sprinted toward the smoke wall and casualties while

With smoke in the background concealing movement. SGT Kiel looks down at a pool of blood on the rock with a wounded Afghan Army soldier.

dodging incoming sniper fire that was being sporadically sprayed through the smoke. Jumping from ledges onto rocks and up hills, we ran as fast as we could in a unified direction looking for the scattered bodies of the wounded.

"I got one wounded Afghan Soldier right here!" SFC Eagan shouted.

On a single hill completely exposed, I saw an Afghan soldier laying with his legs up and a arm behind his head begging for help. My team leader, SGT Kiel, pointed at him and instructed me to work on him while he ran forward to help others. I took a knee in a pool of blood and looked for his injuries when something poked me in my leg. I looked down to see his femur bone sticking to my pants. I maneuvered around him and saw a huge hole in the side of his calf exposing his broken bone and discharged maimed muscle. I placed a tourniquet onto his leg and realigned his bone to reset it from preventing further damage. I then finished up by shoving as much gauze that I had into his wound and secured the area with an Israeli pressure dressing. As I wrote the time of placement on the tourniquet, incoming friendly rockets from the Kiowa helicopters streamed across the sky and landed on the other side of the draw. Little did we know at the time, but we had small pockets of enemy fighters surrounding us and attempting to enclose us in the draw with no exit.

"Water, water, Sir," the wounded Afghan soldier begged.

"I don't have water man, just relax," I replied.

Jesus, what the hell is going on. I got snipers to my front, enemies surrounding my sides, blood is staining my hands and I don't know how we are going to get these wounded down the mountain with Taliban fighters scattered around us.

Where's LT Parten? Jesus. I can't believe he's gone.

Focus Ambriz,. Get this casualty packaged up, move onto the next one. My mind is all over the place. Wake up Ambriz!

"You get this guy down the mountain," I yelled at a random Afghan soldier watching me work. I moved around to grab his legs when I heard screaming behind me and the muffled sound of loose rocks and vegetation only to see SGT Kiel and CPL Systo appear to be dragging the body of my LT.

"He's gone brother," Systo said.

"Someone has to get him off my foot right now," SGT Kiel said out of breath.

Before I could make my way over to help with the LT, off to my left I saw two hands grab a boulder. The bloody hands belonged to SSG Russel, a Cavalry Scout Squad Leader, who was a man the size of bigfoot's testicles, standing easily six foot three inches, 220 pounds without gear. He was crawling toward me crying in pain with a trail of blood behind him on the dirt path. I ran over to him and rolled his body over to see where he was wounded.

"I can't. I can't do it. Leave me," he cried out.

"Shut up Sergeant, you're fine. We are going to get you down," I said.

I looked down to see his lower jaw exposed. He had gotten shot in the mouth and could barely talk without choking on his own blood or swallowing his own tongue. Blood was even more persistent in his legs and I noticed because of his size, he had two tourniquets, but one had come loose. I lay him flat on the ground and gave him a look indicating to him I was going to cause him some pain. Standing over him, I placed my knee onto his femoral artery and twisted his second tourniquet down. The harder I twisted, the harder the blood-choked scream went. I finally sat him up, but because of my smaller stature, it caused him even more pain. It was killing me that I was putting him in so much pain. I had to remind myself as a medic, you couldn't think about their pain. You had to not care, because the priority became keeping them alive. For the first time, not only as a soldier, but also as a man, I didn't know what to do to make the situation better. It just felt like no matter what I did we weren't going to win this one. CPL Systo and SGT Kiel saw our slow movement and came over to help by taking him from me.

As soon as I handed over SSG Russel, I adjusted my helmet and caught my breath only to hear a voice yell, "Someone has to grab LT's body."

Silence… No one moved.

"I'll do it," I replied.

Time seemed to pause while my chest started to hurt as my heart was pounding against my body armor. I took my first steps toward the LT. With my legs trembling as they slid on loose rocks under my boots. *I can't believe I'm about to do this. I don't want to see him like this. I don't have a choice though… I have to help.*

Why can't I hear the guitar anymore?
Wake up.

As I approached the LT, I stared at his face for a moment while telepathically apologizing to him that this had happened. After grabbing his shoulder straps, I pulled up, lifted his back off the ground and slowly dragged him toward the donkey trail. Moving his body carefully took some time as we were trying to be as respectful as we could in a moment like that.

"Ambriz, what are you doing? You have to hurry and move his body," 1SG Wallace yelled.

"First Sergeant, I'm trying. I don't want to drag his head," I replied. "Jesus…"

SFC Eagan yelled, "Everyone hurry, the smoke is going to clear!"

I tried to muster up as much adrenaline as I could. I pulled on his vest and dug into the ground to ensure I could get his body back. Screaming through the pain of muscle fatigue and running out of breath. I finally reached the rock wall and collapsed next to the LT's body. Lying next to him with my face against the ground, and eyes closed, I inhaled dirt, released a cough and looked up to lock eyes with LT Parten. *I'm sorry Sir, I am so sorry. I love you.* Looking up on the path, I saw my leaders formulating the next phase to our plan. We started to reconsolidate the gear and weapons of the wounded to lessen the load and burden on their injuries. I slung five weapons across my back and awaited orders from my NCOs. The dense and rigid terrain route we took on the way up was too much for the wounded and KIA to be carried down. First sergeant instructed me to follow him and be the lead element for the reconnaissance mission in finding a trail down the mountain. I looked back at the LT and paused for a moment, because I knew it would be the last time I was ever going to see him.

In the middle of a firefight, we never really thought about death because we knew it was a part of the daily routine in war; but when someone was killed, it made our heart sink. We would start to question about when our time was coming. We would start to visualize how it would happen. Would it be painful? Would it be quick? This type of thinking didn't do anybody any good, it only distracted us from trying to survive.

"Ambriz, let's go!" 1SG Wallace yelled.

The lead element consisted of first sergeant, SGT Lee, a cavalry scout, an Afghan interpreter, and me. The middle element consisted of multiple Afghan Army soldiers carrying the wounded soldier I had worked on. The trail element carried our wounded and the LT. It was dark enough for our night vision goggles to be completely ineffective, not only with the poor moonlight, but also Murphy's Law ensured our brand-new batteries were dying. Kicking rocks off ledges was the only way we could determine how far a drop was. Each ledge and ravine brought us new courses of action on how we were getting the wounded down a way we had never seen before. Although movement was slow, it was quiet, and we were no longer taking fire from the enemy.

Almost midway down the mountain, a bright light shined at our feet from behind us. We spun around to see an Afghan Army soldier impatiently fumbling with his flashlight. His bright light was exposing our position and silhouetting our bodies to Saw village directly across from us.

"Tell him to turn that light off, now!" 1SG Wallace yelled.

I turned around and started to run back up the hill to grab the flashlight, but two steps in, our world got lit up. The entire village as well as two additional fighting positions on the adjacent mountains opened fire onto our mountainside. It sounded like a thousand cracks and snaps all around our heads while the air was filled with tracers flying in the direction of us. Everyone immediately jumped to the ground and covered the wounded for safety. I slid down a path along the side of a small rock wall. With the first sergeant in between my legs and SGT Lee above me, our interpreter collapsed on my body and told me he was shot. I pulled him close to me and placed a pressure dressing on his wound. As we lay there, it seemed like an hour of nonstop enemy fire pounding at our position and we couldn't do anything but sit there and take it. As I lay there, I felt like my body was being pegged with rocks falling from the sky. Looking up from my back, a Kiowa helicopter was hovering about 50 feet above us and was engaging with his machine gun while hundreds of pieces of his brass rained down on our bodies.

"...Roger, this is Coldblood 7, I am requesting BROKEN ARROW! We need whatever air support you got or else we aren't making it down this mountain!" 1SG Wallace yelled in the radio. Broken Arrow is a term that was used in the Vietnam era and is known in the military for a unit that is on the verge of being overrun or overwhelmed and needs all air support assets to their location.

Broken Arrow? Doesn't that mean everything is going to shit? Sure feels like it at this point. I hope they can bring help.

Ugh, I'm so tired. Everything is getting really dizzy; I wish I had some water.

I feel comfortable laying on this ground, everything feels so light.

Maybe if I close my eyes for just a minute I can think more clearly.

That's when everything went dark...

Wake up!

As I laid there, I lost all consciousness of sound and sight. It was as if I was not even there. I couldn't explain what I was seeing or feeling. It wasn't a dream and it wasn't a mirage. I saw nothing but an image of LT Parten in front of me smiling, I knew he wasn't real and no words were said; nevertheless it felt like I was in the presence of his *ghost* or soul. I had so many thoughts running through my head-so many questions, and no answers. As fast as I saw him, he disappeared just as fast, and I was brought back down into the valley.

I don't know how much time had passed, but when I reopened my eyes, I was greeted with enemy tracers flying over my head and impacting all around us. Sound slowly came back and I started to realize I had reached heat exhaustion and my body was giving out on me. I laid there looking up at the sky with tracers flying in every direction and all I could think about was death. I don't know how we made it this far and I definitely didn't think we were going to get off the mountain. We were stuck, and I was on the verge of accepting my fate. Although I thought about death and the inevitable end that was about to come, my leaders did not. I had to remember how they kept thinking what the next move was to get us out, snapped me out of it. As I came to, I looked up the mountain to see an Afghan soldier making his way down toward us when he froze, looked up, and took two bullets to his face. As his body collapsed, I started to roll over so I could grab him, but his leg was stuck between two rocks and I could not reach him without completely exposing myself.

As my body was half exposed, I looked back across to Saw village to see our trucks engaging the enemy, but was confronted with an odd object. I saw a red ball from the adjacent mountain coming toward our location and getting bigger. An incoming rocket slammed right into the mountain below our rock wall causing shrapnel and rock fragments to pepper the entire area as well as my body. The falling rock and shrapnel dislocated my right shoulder. I screamed in pain, but did not have time to assess it as 1SG Wallace was pushing us down the route. I slid down the next rock embankment followed by SGT Lee, who accidentally kicked a rock onto my already wounded shoulder, further dislocating and injuring it. I screamed in pain again and told SGT Lee he had to reset my shoulder or else I wouldn't be able to carry all the weapons back down. Laying on a rock in the wide open where we were both completely exposed, incoming enemy fire all around us, I told him to hurry. Since there was no other way for him to reset my shoulder with our gear on, he took the buttstock of his rifle and repeatedly slammed it on my shoulder until it reset back into the socket. Probably not the most medically recommended way, it's all we had in the moment and the pain got me back on my feet to continue our recon mission.

As we continued down the mountain, the incoming fire ceased for a moment—they probably reloaded and redistributed ammunition. Then, the loud and thunderous explosion of two 500-pound guided bombs landed on the opposite mountains from an F-16. The good news was some Taliban fighters met their maker, the bad news was the explosion illuminated the entire area and exposed SGT Lee and myself in the open. Saw village watched us crossing this opening and opened fire on the both of us. I jumped in between two boulders and tucked myself away while I watched enemy fire smack against the boulders protecting me. I witnessed a group of Afghan soldiers carry the wounded Afghan I worked on, except he looked a lot less conscious. I ran over to assess the casualty again and noticed they removed the tourniquet because they said he was complaining it hurt.

"It's supposed to hurt, you idiot! Do not remove it again." I reestablished the tourniquet.

I followed the Afghans to ensure they got my patient down the mountain safely. I was one of the first back down on the road where I cracked a chemlight and placed it on the path for others to follow. I immediately walked over to SSG Brown, who was at my squad leader's truck to inform him I was back down for accountability purposes. I started to slowly walk back to my truck when I was confronted by SPC Patsky, a friend of mine from the squad, who gave me a big hug.

"Hey bro, are you okay?" he asked.

"I'm going to say yeah, but I don't know I think I'm lying to you at this point," I replied.

Whoop… whoop… whoop… whoop, the sound of rippling based blades could be heard overhead. A Blackhawk helicopter was hovering over the mountain I just came from hoisting the wounded and LT Parten back to FOB Bostick. I was about to head back to my truck and wait for the others when Patsky and I looked ahead on the road and saw a lone American walking by himself in the open. It was dark so I couldn't make it out at first, but I could see his body armor completely open, his chinstrap undone and his weapon dangling, practically being dragged on the dirt road. It was CPL Systo, who walked over to us and immediately collapsed in our arms. I looked around his body for any bullet holes, but did not see any. After getting him some water, I sat him against the truck tire and took his helmet off. He just stared past me with that thousand-yard stare like he had seen a *ghost*.

"Systo, you gotta let me know what happened. Look at me. Tell me Corporal."

"When we started to get shot at, I slid off the mountain to the left. I got separated from everyone. On my way down I heard people speaking and it wasn't English. I thought it was the Afghan soldiers, but they weren't," he replied.

"Wait, you ran into the Taliban? How close were you to them?"

SGT Kiel, PFC Sherbino, PFC Ambriz, CPL Systo, 2009.

"Fifteen or 20 feet. I had to ditch some of my gear and hide between a rock pile until they left. I thought they were going to get me man."

"But, they didn't. You're here with us. Come on Corporal, sit in the truck and relax," I said.

I had about enough for the day so I walked back to my truck, opened the back and sat down. I took my helmet off and took a deep breath. I hadn't sipped on water since SFC Eagan shared his with me six hours before. I felt around in the back of the truck searching for a water bottle, because they had all fallen on the floor and were scattered. I picked up the first one I could find, opened the cap, and when that first drop hit my lip…

Yup. That's my urine.

My piss bottle from earlier that morning just happened to get thrown in the back and was the random one I chose to mouthwash with. At this point in the day, I would expect nothing less with how it should've ended. I just wanted to close my eyes and forget any of this ever happened.

Once everybody was off the mountain, we got accountability of all personnel and weapons and were told to return to base. I used my one good arm to drive the vehicle back to base since my right shoulder was in too much pain. Once at the gate, SGT Kiel rushed me to the aid station to get looked at. As I opened the door to the aid station, all of my medic buddies were working on the casualties that came from the mountain. My helmet chinstrap was undone, hanging next to my face, my vest was completely open, and I was barely holding onto my rifle in my good arm. I stared out in front, front of me, looking lost.

"Ambriz, you good?" SGT Moore asked, looking concerned while reaching for me.

Starting to process the seriousness of what had happened I looked to the left and saw LT Parten covered with a blanket. I started to cry and returned my eyes to SGT Moore. "I'm hit Sergeant," I said.

As my body was completely giving out on me, I collapsed into SGT Moore's arms, not wanting to do anything anymore. A few of the other medics dragged me into another room and ripped my gear off of me and cut my uniform open to tend to my wounds. I laid there on the litter hearing the chaos of the aid station while looking at the ceiling completely dazed as they started to x-ray my shoulder. To my right, a brand-new replacement medic who just got in the country was staring at me, and I stared right back at him. I realized I was giving him that same rare vacant stare those medics once gave me when I first walked into the aid station. I knew now that I had seen the unforgettable.

Wake up.

This was only a prelude for the Taliban, who a month later initiated the deadliest battle in Afghanistan against the 3/61 Cavalry Regiment (the unit I was attached to) just twenty miles to the north of our location. On the morning of October 3, 2009, an estimated 300–400 Taliban fighters assaulted COP Keating completely surrounded the base and overrunning it. The enemy entered the through wire and would have engulfed the entire base had it not been for a group of brave Americans who pushed the enemy out of the area. When the battle was over, my good friend from Fort Carson, SPC Mace, was killed along with seven others. The decorations themselves explained the outcome of the battle as seven Distinguished Flying Crosses, twenty-seven Purple Hearts, thirty-seven Army Commendation Medals with "V" device for valor, three Bronze Star Medals, eighteen Bronze Star Medals with "V" device for valor, eight Silver Stars, one Distinguished Service Cross, and two Medal of Honors.

September 10, 2009. What a day to remember! I saw a half a dozen Noncommissioned Officers come together, lead a rescue mission, and overcome incredible feats. Being the youngest one during that operation that day, I learned a lot through their actions that have been major building blocks to my leadership style.

Selflessness and duty drove me every day just as I witnessed all those years ago. LT Parten was an amazing leader, who was kindhearted with a beautiful soul. He was taken too soon. A piece of all of us died on that mountain with him that day. A part of us will forever roam that valley as ghosts still searching for him to try and warn him of the dangers ahead.

Wake up LT!

LT Tyler Parten

6 The Rucksacks Purpose
May 2010 – April 2011
Fort Carson, Colorado

"Attention to orders!"

"To all who shall see these presents, greeting: This is to certify that the President of the United States of America authorized by executive order, 24 August 1962 has awarded the Bronze Star Medal with Valor device to Private First Class Sean T. Ambriz. For valorous actions and meritorious actions while engaged in direct combat operations in support of Operation Enduring Freedom on 10 September 2009. Private First Class Ambriz's courage and selfless dedication in a combat zone, under the most extreme circumstances, greatly contributed to the fight against the war on terrorism. Private First Class Ambriz's actions reflect great credit upon himself, Task Force Mountain Warrior, Combined Joint Task Force-82 and the United States Central Command, signed Curtis M. Scaparrotti, Major General, US Army, Commanding.

This isn't right. I don't want this. I just want LT Parten back. God damn it, here comes the battalion commander. There are so many people here.

Wake up!

Snapping to, I stood at the position of attention, looking straight ahead at the group of individuals attending our award ceremony. I felt lifeless, as lifeless as I was on that mountain. I could not move and had no say in the matter. As my battalion commander walked over to me, we locked eyes. He mumbled words I will never remember. I could not focus on anything but the burden he was about to bestow upon me. My hands were dripping with sweat and my legs were starting to lock up as his left hand grabbed the collar of my uniform and with the right, he pinned a Bronze Star medal with

Valor and Purple Heart on my chest. As he released the awards, I felt a huge weight pulling on my chest as I now carried the responsibility of the award, as well as the weight of LT Parten's death.

MPs receive awards for service

Story and photo by
Geoffrey Roper
Mountaineer staff

Leaders from the 759th Military Police Battalion presented individual awards and campaign medals during an end-of-tour awards ceremony held at the Special Events Center May 26.

The ceremony honored and acknowledged the work and accomplishments of Soldiers from the Headquarters and Headquarters Company, 759th MP Bn., and 984th Military Police Company, during their yearlong deployment to Afghanistan in support of Operation Enduring Freedom.

Soldiers from the 759th MP Bn. conducted combined operations with the Afghan border police and Afghan national police, and the 984th MP Company worked closely with the Afghan national police. Both units were stationed in Nuristan, Nngarhar, Kunar and Lagman provinces.

More than 200 Family members, friends and other Soldiers came out to show their support to the troops given awards.

"The Soldiers in the battalion, they have a great sense of pride, and this is just a reflection of their mentality as they go about their mission," said Sgt. Samuel Morgan, 759th MP Bn.

The battalion was constituted in August 1942 and activated that September at Fort Ontario, N.Y. It relocated to Fort Carson in 1987. It has participated in campaigns from WWII all the way up to current times in Afghanistan.

The highest award presented during the ceremony went to Spc. Sean

Ambriz, who received a Bronze Star Medal with Valor and a Purple Heart.

Civilians working in support of the battalion also received awards and recognition during the ceremony.

Some received The President's Volunteer Service Award, which is presented to those who have volunteered their personal time to help the unit, Fort

Spc. Sean Ambriz, 759th Military Police Battalion, receives his Purple Heart and Bronze Star Medal with Valor, during the end-of-tour awards ceremony held at the Special Events Center May 26.

Carson and the Army as a whole. Volunteers are awarded based on how many hours they have given.

Others received Heart of the Mountain Awards, given to Family members who have given outstanding volunteer service to the Fort Carson community while their spouses were deployed.

After the ceremony was complete, local news crews shoved their lights and cameras in my face as I stood there mouth open, and at a loss for words. The interview felt like an interrogation. I asked to have 1LT Nichoson stand with me because I didn't feel comfortable answering any questions alone. I wasn't sure how to answer some of the questions, because how do you explain something like that at nineteen years old? I didn't even know how to process it for myself, let alone explain it.

What do I do now?

I yearned for the brotherhood and simplistic life again and felt lost without it. I understand the demand combat weighs on the human body and mind, but performing at these levels was something we searched for. I soon realized that, back home, I could no longer find a job that required the gamble of life and death. Coming home left me with a sense of emptiness, as I walked into my newly assigned barracks room that was completely empty, minus a pillow and wool blanket, provided by the unit. The family readiness group was nice enough to leave a pillow cover customized with the 984th and MP company guidon on the cover as well as a goodie bag full of chips and snacks. We had to wait a week or so until our items could be removed from storage and delivered, so until then, we survived off of whatever we had. Deathly silent in the barracks room I pushed the wool blanket to the left and I set my back against the cold brick wall, ate a bag of chips in silence, and tried to figure out what was next after all of this.

Being back home didn't feel right knowing we still had soldiers in Afghanistan needing help. I didn't normally do much with others and found myself going from being around a group of individuals every day, to spending the majority of my day alone. I drove around to get my mind off of things, which didn't help leaving the main gate to Fort Carson our first month back and seeing a new welcome party. The Westboro Baptist Church, famously known for their hate speech, is against gays, Jews, Muslims, politicians, and US soldiers. *Yeah, real winners.* A group of them drove from Kansas where they are headquartered out of, holding signs and making statements such as, "Thank God for IEDs" and "The Best Soldiers, are Dead Soldiers." I didn't know what to think when I first saw it. Others were extremely upset, naturally, and wanted to retaliate, but that just wasn't how I was raised. Somewhere there's a piece of paper that says I fought for their right to say whatever they would like, so who am I to stop them. It was acts like these that started me to retrograde into my own personal foxhole away from the public. I just wanted to keep to myself.

Most of our weekends consisted of the same things prior to the deployment. I would DD the guys from downtown and we would stay up late to exchange war stories from the previous deployment until we fell asleep playing Call of Duty. We were just trying to fill the void, since it couldn't be filled at this point.

My adjustment coming back home was about as straight as scoliosis. I wanted to talk to somebody and get everything off my chest, but I had no one to go to. At least that's what I thought, even though I had plenty of leaders and friends. *I just don't want to be deemed weak.* I didn't know what to even say that could make everything better. I don't think my family fully accepted the threshold I had just walked through. They knew I deployed and that there was some fighting, but to an extent it might as well have been small pop shots. They never really knew the full details and I guess they'll never really know all the stories. Even if I ever did tell them, a part of them probably wouldn't even accept it. I'm their baby boy. There's no way I could have gone through something like that. A piece of them doesn't want to accept that their little altar boy from church is somehow ruined.

How could I ever tell them? Who do I even talk to if they're not going to understand?

I figured I talked to nobody else more than myself throughout the day so why not just keep it to myself and try to process it all. Yeah, real genius I was. I should've utilized the military resources and reached out and got some help, but I did the minimal rehab possible. The doctors I did see were good and they were able to spot some deficiencies with my mental health early, but it was a two-way street and I just wasn't budging. The doctors diagnosed me with Traumatic Brain Injury (TBI) and Post-Traumatic Stress Disorder (PTSD). Like most guys who return from war where they saw some type of real fighting, this was all normal to them. I almost didn't want to accept it myself and couldn't believe that I was somehow weak and labeled by these disorders.

So does this mean I'm not a fit soldier?

I tried going against the grain and told them they were wrong even though I went to sleep every night with a burning rage in my chest and I woke up every morning with my mind running on pure anxiety. I tried to remain positive, I tried to think about what my brother Tony would do or what he would say to make light of the situation through his positive attitude, but nothing was working.

Moments of silence throughout my days brought me nothing but vivid memories of the aid station. All I pictured were the casualties' faces, mopping up blood after numerous mass casualty events, and carrying dead bodies to the freezers.

I thought about LT Parten, wishing I could hear him sing and play the guitar. The only image I kept seeing was his face when I was lying next to him in the dirt. The thing is, I didn't want to not think about him, even if it was like that. I never wanted to forget him or those images. I felt as if those moments and times were making me into who I was.

I wanted to talk about what happened on that day in the mountains and explain LT Parten's sacrifices so that people would understand what he gave up. I just didn't know how. I was told by an old mentor that If you don't remember somebody out loud they die twice. The problem was that everything was building inside of me, which wasn't healthy. It felt as if the boogeyman was in my closet and he couldn't get out. One thing I found out very quickly was that trying to fix PTSD was like jumping rope without a rope—you're jumping all right, but are you really doing it without the rope

So yeah, I was trying to get fixed, but was I actually getting fixed?

Remember that look those medics gave me when I first walked in the aid station? That thousand-yard stare I once got from them. I was seeing that a lot myself every passing day.

I didn't even recognize myself anymore. I couldn't sleep. Every twenty minutes throughout the night, I woke up just to look around and see where I was at and make sure that my surrounding area was safe. I was just always anxious about everything around me.

The next few months slowly ate at me with the boring repetitive work schedule, and a bunch of bad decisions that left me with nothing in my bank account. I just tried to find something to make me feel alive, but nothing seemed to bring excitement into my life; nothing made me feel more alive than the killing fields. I started to lose sight of reality and my purpose.

Purpose? What the hell is my purpose anymore?

I did my job, now I'm back. Now what? Sit here and rot?

Jesus, what if I no longer have a purpose?

My Battalion Commander, LTC Heberer, tried to keep my mind at ease and use my experiences as a platform for the Military Police Corps, which I didn't mind because as a solder, it was my job to be a representation of the corps. I was selected to be All-American and attend the US Army All-Star football game with ninety other soldiers chosen throughout the entire army. The game was hosted by the army every year and sponsored the top high school football athletes prior to their college announcements and debut. Each soldier chosen had to be a recipient of a Purple Heart or some sort of valorous award and were there to represent the army during a time of war. It felt like the older days when valor award recipients were used to showcase to the public for war bonds, except we were there for the country's morale.

For a week, each soldier was partnered with a football player and would escort a player to each event. Each soldier also served as a sponsor and adult life mentor. It was an amazing opportunity and event that included meeting the Chief of Staff, Sergeant Major of the Army, and Medal of Honor recipient SSG Salvatore Giunta. During the game's halftime, I stood next to my football player and his family as he announced he was attending LSU next semester. Seeing everyone fill up with emotions while excited by this young man's career about to bloom was nice to watch and gave me a sense of fulfillment that my deployment had meant something.

Oh yeah, the football player I sponsored and was with during his announcement was Odell Beckham Jr. Youtube "Odell Beckham Nike commercial" and spot your boy at fourteen seconds in.

Odell Beckham Jr announcing his college decision during the US Army All-Star game.

Back at Fort Carson, SFC Lyle had started to prepare me for this competition called the Military Police Warfighter, which essentially was the MP version of the Best Ranger competition. Where the top MPs from all over the Army representing their installation would go to Fort Leonard Wood, Missouri and conduct a three-day competition for bragging rights for being the best MPs in the corps. For two months, we trained every single day on the basic soldier tasks as well as some advanced functions. The most crucial part was our physical fitness, which was pushed to the edge daily as we conducted physical training twice a day. We would also hike up Colorado Springs famous Pikes Peak mountain twice a week, which stands at 14,115 feet and is one of the United States top 100 highest peaks. I was in the best physical shape I could've been at that point in my life and I felt fully prepared with the team that we had assembled for the competition.

Three-man teams were comprised of an NCO and two soldiers. You had to conduct every task and drill as a team, and you could be no more than 10 feet from your teammates at any time. During the three-day competition, we would average two to three hours of sleep per night

Warfighter Competition 2010.

and over 20 miles of rucking per day. It was one of the most physically demanding events I've ever endured, but it was very rewarding being surrounded by some of the top military police in the Army. On day three, we were sitting in the mud as it was raining down on us and the commandant of the military police corps, Brigadier General (Retired) David D. Phillips, walked up to a group of us in his nice crisp uniform and gave us a big, "Good morning warfighters!"

"Careful Sir, you don't want to get that nice uniform dirty now," a soldier said laughing.

"Dirty? Watch this shit." He sat down in the mud next to us. He continued to scoop mud from the ground and rub it deep into his uniform, all over his legs and his torso.

SPC Mendes and SPC Ambriz after the competition

"Don't think I forgot where I came from, warrior." He smirked.

"Yes Sir," we yelled back!

As he stood up to walk away in his freshly shit-covered uniform, he turned around and said, "Listen, you all are my Warfighters. If any of you, and I mean *any* of you need anything, you come see me directly."

Shit. I might have to take you up on that Sir.

Long story short, we should've come in first place, but we placed in seventh, because our NCO quit on us during the last event. Now I don't hold grudges or try to sacrifice people, so I refuse to say his name and what exactly happened, because that was between our team. Regardless, it was a lesson learned and something that I do not regret enduring.

When we returned to Fort Carson, my command sergeant major

My father receiving a pin from General Phillips.

was extremely proud of how we conducted ourselves and represented our unit. He asked me and the other soldier, SPC Threadgill, what military school we wanted. We had open reigns to pick whatever we dreamt of—airborne, air assault, RANGER!

Yep, that's it, Ranger. Nothing else mattered. All I ever wanted was to either be a Ranger or attend Ranger school.

"Ranger school, Sergeant Major," we announced.

"Okay, done. You boys got it, I will have the school's NCO look at the next available dates for you to attend and get back to you. In the meantime, I'm pulling both of you out of the line unit and letting you rest for a bit. I'm going to send you over to the detachment to be a part of the special reaction team (SRT)," he said.

SRT was usually made fun of by other MPs, but that's because they were either too unfit or had a bad experience with a previous SRT and just wanted to make fun of it. SRT was essentially the Army's version of a SWAT and we were the on-call tactical law-enforcement unit for the installation commander. The team normally was comprised of ten to twenty members and had an entry team as well as a Marksman Observer (sniper) team. The SRT provided the commander enhanced response capabilities of conventional tactical law-enforcement and security patrols and they would respond to resolve high-risk incidents such as a terrorist incident, barricaded subject (with or without hostages), a drug raid, high-risk warrant apprehension, or an active shooters.

Hate on it all you want; it's a badass job!

After being on the team for two weeks, I was sent to Fort Leonard Wood to attend special reaction team school so that I could be certified to actually conduct live missions with the team. During the two-week school, the Army released its promotion points for sergeant, which I made. Being the impatient person that I am, I did not want to have to wait another week and a half or so to get pinned the rank and I wanted to wear it at that moment.

Wait a minute. General Phillips told me back in Warfighter, whatever I wanted. Well looks like I can take him up on that.

Side note: Walking into the regimental corridor that holds some of the highest ranking individuals in the Military Police Corps with a little to no plan-no bueno.

As I walked in, with a stern look on my face. I stared at the civilian secretary to my left who looked at me with a confused look on her face.

"Can I help you?" she asked.

"Yes ma'am. I need to see General Phillips."

"Uh, are you on his calendar, because that's kind of how it works," she responded.

Leaning my arm against her table and in a whispering manner I said, *like a douchebag*, "Ma'am, I am one of his Warfighters. He said to come see him whenever I needed him. So, here I am."

Hearing the fuss from the hallway, General Phillips peaked his head around the corner, recognized me, and asked what I was doing there. I told him that I made points for sergeant and that I was attending SRT school here. Since I didn't have any of my leadership present, I was inquiring whether or not he could pin my new rank on me. Surprisingly, he was ecstatic to do so. He stopped what he was doing and told his entire staff to stop and come to the conference room to watch me pin on sergeant. He had his admin clerk run and generate the orders as well as produce new rank for my uniform and within thirty minutes he had a ceremony ready to go. As we stood in the conference room listening to the admin clerk, he announced the orders appointing me to the rank of sergeant. It was at that point, I realized how bad I was going to get smoked later by my leadership.

Worth it!

As my specialist rank was ripped from my chest and sergeant was placed there, I had a flashback of my deployment. My moment of joy shifted to a moment of seriousness. I thought about my NCOs, SFC Eagan, 1SG Wallace, SGT Kiel, CPL Systo, SFC Lyle, and many others. Moments with them and the experiences they shared with me hit me in a reminder that I was now taking on the responsibility they once held. I was no longer just a soldier. I now had the responsibility of maturing into a leader as I would soon be handed soldiers of my own. After the ceremony was complete, General Phillips kicked everyone out of the conference room so that it was just me, him, and the command sergeant major.

"You see this flag you are standing next to, Sergeant?" he asked.

I looked to my left and saw an American flag that looked discolored, burnt, and not well-kept.

"This flag was in the Pentagon on September 11th. It was burning, so I ran back in and grabbed it. You just got promoted with a piece of history, son," he said.

Promotion to Sergeant with General Phillips, 2010.

I couldn't believe it. I felt so honored to even be in a room with such individuals who literally watched history in the making. When I was in my room at the age of twelve, I watched the events of September 11th on TV with my dad. Now, I was standing with a man who lived it. Years later, I never thought this universe would bring us together in that moment, inducting me into the leader ranks. I knew my maneuver to get promoted by the commandant was a ballsy one, but it was one that I will remember for the rest of my life.

Once I returned to Fort Carson, it was time for me to start building myself as a leader and train numerous hours in my new job as a member of the SRT. During my first month after graduating SRT school, we conducted fake callouts, which essentially tested our reaction time when the team received

Explosive Breached Training, Schofield Barracks, Hawaii, 2016.

a phone call for a possible incident. This tested our response time to get to our stations and gear up for whatever incident it may be. When on the team, you had certain days you could not drink or go out of a certain mileage away from base to help with our reaction time. We rehearsed callouts multiple times throughout the week and at various times to test our team's flexibility. With anything, the more you test it, the better you get; but if you do it too much, you also cry wolf. For example while I was in SRT school an individual who had multiple warrants and felonies came to Fort Carson and decided to rob the Burger King on the installation. In the process of his robbery, he shot the manager in the shoulder and fled the scene. Criminal investigations detachment published a $5,000 reward for his whereabouts. We received a call at 5 a.m. In December 2010 that didn't show any signs of distress or anxiousness. So we arrived at the detachment and figured it was like any other drill until we sat in the briefing room and there were multiple FBI agents present along with live ammunition sitting on the table.

What the hell is going on?

A picture of the suspect was placed on the screen and we were briefed that his location had been given up by one of his friends for the $5,000 reward. The suspect was staying on post housing with a pregnant soldier in one of the units. Once we prepared all of our gear and formulated a plan, we staged on a hill overlooking the

Joint Special Operations Room Clearing Training, Schofield Barracks, Hawaii, 2017.

community with the battalion commander and the joint task force put together by the installation commander. Standing outside the incident command post, three vehicles, two Honda Civics, and one gutted out soccer mom car, pulled up with tinted windows. Military police patrols blocked off the surrounding neighborhood and were in the process of notifying the local elementary school that was about to dismiss. The battalion even had undercover military police roaming the streets in civilian clothes to create the ruse that nothing in particular was going on.

Well this is definitely different. It felt so weird looking down in between my legs having my M4 carbine locked and loaded on a military installation and possibly having to use it on American citizens. This is not like Afghanistan. Trying to switch my mindset from combat to law enforcement was one that I was fighting with at that moment.

SSG Ambriz on the right. Koko Head Range, Hawaii, 2017.

Once granted authorization from the installation commander, we mounted up into the vehicles and drove toward the target building. On cue, we initiated movement toward the residence. Since I was one of the newer members, myself and SGT Exline were in charge of the rear corridor of the home. Upon our approach, an individual walked out the back door of the house and locked eyes with me. So much for being the new guy and not coming in contact with the suspect. Before I could get a command out of my mouth, the individual ran back into the home. Simultaneously, our entry team was at the front door ready to make the breach. Once they started to cross the threshold into the doorway, they saw a little girl sitting on the couch so they decided to throw the flash bang at their own feet instead of toward the child. After the flash bang exploded, the entry team was so fast on their movements the suspect was not able to run back inside from the back door and retrieve the weapons that were sitting next to the child. We were able to apprehend the suspect with no shots fired and a successful raid complete.

Well that was definitely a different type of adrenaline rush.

SRT Snipers overwatch 4th of July event on 25th Infantry Headquarters building, 2017.

A week later, the installation commander recognized our team with coins of excellence. As much fun as I was having with a different type of experience seeing the world in a law enforcement capacity for the first time, I had to leave it.

"Hey Ambriz, did you hear they're looking for volunteers in the 127th military police company to go Afghanistan?" a friend of mine asked.

Releasing a happy nervous fart.

"Don't play with my emotions. Are they really?" I replied.

"Yeah man, and they really need leaders. Since you just pinned sergeant, I know you want to go back. Maybe this is your opportunity?"

The 127th MP Company was a sister company to the one I had just returned from. They needed leaders with experience and seeing as most of the company had no combat experience, it was my duty, volunteer. Some would say, I did my time, I already went, why go back? Look, I know guys who have up to a dozen deployments under their belt. I will continue to go as long as I have something to give. That's my duty. That's what my NCOs on that mountain in September would have done. So, I'm doing it.

I went straight to my sergeant major and told him that I wanted to deploy with the 127th. He was ecstatic that he had leaders willing to come forward and go do the Lord's work in a sense. Problem was, the Ranger school slot he promised me was around the same month that I would be deploying. Since I was volunteering for the deployment and he had promised me the school, he was leaving it up to me as to which one I wanted. Ranger school obviously was something no one could ever take away from me. Going to endure the toughest leadership school the military had to offer was something I wanted more than anything else in this world. At the same time, I signed to serve my country and deploy, so who knew how many more deployments would be coming my way with the way the war was going. It would've killed me if I went to Ranger school only to be peer dropped because I was an MP or if I was injured and missed out on both of the school and deployment. It was one of the hardest decisions I had to make, but I knew it was right to pick the deployment and lead soldiers in combat. Taking what I had learned from my deployment and giving back to others was what my NCOs did for me when I first got to the unit. Now it was my duty and obligation. After I volunteered for the second deployment, I just had to wait for the dwell time paperwork to be approved. Usually, when you return from a deployment, you are placed in a twelve-month dwell time, which is a reset window for soldiers to decompress and then prepare for the next deployment. I was sitting at my eight-month window when I met my now wife, Aimee.

"No way, you were in the Hooters calendar, right?" I asked.

"Yes." She said with a smile.

"You were hanging on my wall above my head during my last deployment," I replied while fully aware that I sounded like a Justin Bieber fan.

Months later I finally mustered up enough courage to ask her on a date to a restaurant called Old Chicago. She didn't know that I didn't drink alcohol and she was one that could definitely throw them back. As we sat at the bar, we talked and discussed our lives doing the basic question and answer thing back and forth to get a feel for one another. After the restaurant closed up, we started to head toward the parking lot. I still had yet to try and make a move in any type of flirtatious manner, as she was completely out of my league. So, as the man she is, she made the first move by giving me a little shove and then laughed.

"Oh, you want to go." I threw my arms in the air.

"Let's go," she said while putting her purse down.

We locked eyes while smiling. It was very intense, waiting to see who would conduct the first move toward our now playful skirmish. So, what did I do? I took two steps toward her, cocked my right leg back and kicked the shit out of her purse, *like a boss.*

With her purse exploding makeup, money, and whatever else women put in their purse, flew in every direction penetrating cars nearby. As my foot came back to the ground, I realized very quickly this may not have been the best flirtatious move I could've come up with. Before I could turn my eyes to her, I looked directly into a police officers eyes who was in a patrol car and had seen the entire event play out in front of him.

Great, this guy thinks that we're going to have a domestic. Best first date, ever!

Luckily, she laughed and somehow found it funny as we started to pick up the 526 things that had come out of her purse. We dated for three months, having fun and getting to know one another. Then, one day I jokingly asked if she wanted to get married. Without hesitation, she responded with "I'll grab the keys." She wasn't one for a big wedding and to waste $10,000 on a wedding dress for one day so we kept it classy and headed down to the Colorado Springs courtroom followed by breakfast at 7-Eleven. It didn't feel right not to have my family there and I know that we were kind of jumping on it quickly, but it felt right between her and I, which I don't regret. Everything was going great in the relationship until I had my first slip up as a husband.

"Ambriz, your dwell time paperwork got kicked back. Since you got married, your wife has to sign the paperwork allowing you to go," my first sergeant said.

Well, shit.

It's one thing to forget the groceries or even take out the trash. It is a whole different thing to forget to tell your spouse you volunteered for war. Not only that, she has to go see the commanding general, face to face, and sign my waiver like it was a school day field trip.

So, after my first night on the couch as a husband, we talked about how we were going to get through this next deployment. I prepared her with all the finances, notes, bills, contact information, and gave her the rundown on how military life worked. She did her best and then some on the home front supporting my team and me.

I had finally found my purpose: doing war shit with my war friends.

Trying to get my mind right and prepare to endure the mental aspects of war was challenging. Attempting to build that same mental strength in my soldiers who had never seen that type of violence was even more challenging. My soldiers had a different agenda than I had. They had the same innocent mindset I embraced going into my first deployment: excited to serve their country and hoping to make a change while gaining experience. I, on the other hand, was going back for revenge and was driven by anger and hate. So the second deployment I knew that if I went with a personal vendetta and not thinking clearly, I could get someone killed, but it was hard not to focus on those we had lost the first time around. As dangerous as it was, the danger is not that you will lose yourself—though that is always possible—but that you will lose sight of the greater purpose of each mission.

Through the thrill of war and by chance of another deployment finding my way, just like that, the rucksack that carried our equipment had been filled with my purpose again. Leading them in combat is my purpose. Through my experiences, I would have to work through the art of command and the science of leadership. Taking my soldiers to war and at all cost, bring them home, alive.

With revenge and rage in my horizon, all I could think about was that it was time to end Taliban bloodlines.

Wake up.

Saying our goodbyes, moments before we get on the bus to Afghanistan, 2011.

7 The Reawakening
April 2011 – April 2012
Nangarhar Province, Afghanistan

For the first three months we conducted missions in and around the city of Jalalabad, Afghanistan, gathering information, conducting community projects, and training the Afghan police. So far, this deployment was nothing like my first; I told stories to my soldiers to prepare them for the worst, but in comparison this seemed like a fairy tale. No major contact with the enemy was made and although I was able to be back and doing something productive, it just wasn't the same. Being in the city, I could look to the north and see the mountains I fought in just a year earlier.

God, I wish I was in those mountains. I'd give anything to get back in the fight there.

As days went by, we were ordered to process the Jalalabad Regional Prison and sort through the over 600 prisoners for intelligence. Most of the days were boring with the repetitiveness of administrative paperwork and forensics checking. As lines of prisoners would come through, I would have to listen to their individual problems as to why they were wrongfully accused, sometimes staring Taliban in the face—which made it worse a hell of a lot worse for me because there was nothing I could do. All that anger and revenge built up in me and I could do nothing but push these people off to the next station. Upon completion of our forensics and police intelligence, we found that the prison was housing over twelve-tier-one HVTs. Most of the police stations in the Jalalabad area were built up because of their geographical radius to the American counterparts, as it was easier for them to acquire funds and assistance. Their stations were nice with built-

SGT Ambriz at the Jalalabad Prison, 2011

in bathrooms; high fence lines; and more importantly, standoff distance with serpentine barriers to prevent any type of vehicle borne IEDs. Physically, they had everything they needed, but mentally their training was weak. They couldn't care less because the attacks in Jalalabad were sporadic and subpar compared to the surrounding outside areas.

My commander, CPT Spence, was a Ranger-tabbed hard ass who was respected by the soldiers and loved to work the hell out of us. Weeks would go by between missions with little to no sleep just to keep a high presence in Jalalabad. Sometimes conducting eight-hour training patrols with the Afghan Police was not enough and as soon as we came back, we had to re-fuel and head back out for another three to four hours on reconnaissance patrols. This may not seem like much, especially since we weren't taking any contact, but it did take a toll on the psychological aspects. Every time we left the base, we instantly felt vulnerable to every aspect in the environment. We trusted nothing and we were never sure that we were going to come back alive. Every piece of trash, broken down car, or fat Afghan just might just be waiting to blow us up so by the time we were done with the five-hour mission we were mentally drained. Of course, soldiers were always going to bitch about being overworked and not getting paid enough to do this. While, they made valid points at times, it was up to me and the other team leaders to hold the squad's integrity together either by explaining the situation, showing them the bigger picture, describing the purpose, or just telling them to shut the hell up.

As for my anger, it wouldn't take long for my wish to come true and release some of that revenge. Going into our fourth month, we received a new replacement squad leader, SSG Castellanos (Cas, as we called him). We knew nothing about him, and it was hard to want to go out and put foot to ass when we knew nothing of our leader. He was particularly quiet initially as he tried to get a feel for his new soldiers and vice versa. On the night of June 5, 2011, SSG Cas and myself had our first thing in common—losing a friend. The day prior in a nearby province, another MP company sustained casualties when a truck hit an IED and killed four MPs. Throughout the night and most of the day, our entire area was on blackout status—meaning, when an American is killed, everyone in the surrounding area is put on a blackout status that disconnects us from the outside world so the news wouldn't leak on social media. No computers or telephones can be used to connect with family back home until the family of the fallen has been notified. This strategy was set in place because of mistakes in the past when families were finding out through social media that they had lost a loved one as opposed to the proper way of being notified by an official notification officer through the Army.

When the blackout was lifted, I went to the computers to check my Facebook and send a message to my wife when I noticed everybody on my feed was saying "RIP Powell."

What? No, this can't be, this has to be a coincidence.

It wasn't. CPL Powell, the hard ass country team leader from my first deployment was killed with three others, one of them SPC Devin Snyder, a good friend of SSG Cas. I found out Powell did the same thing I did. He had left Fort Carson after our first deployment to go to Alaska and as soon as he got there, he volunteered to go back to Afghanistan with another MP company. Someone who endured the same valleys as me on our first deployment, a brother, was killed no more than 10 miles from me, and I had no idea. I couldn't believe I had lost another friend. This one hurt, being how close our platoon was that first deployment. A week later I saw pictures online from my buddies who had served with me during that deployment as they consolidated in Texas for the arrival of Powell's body. I watched as my old brothers buried Powell, and I was stuck in Afghanistan where his soul left the earth. I hated that I could not be a part of it. I held my own ceremony on mission one day where I secluded myself from everyone else behind some mud hut homes of suspected Taliban. I walked around to the alley with no security and gave a few moments of my day to remember him. I pulled out my Gerber utility knife and carved in "RIP Powell" in huge letters against the mud hut wall. I stared at it for about twenty minutes thinking about the events that had happened during my first deployment and where I was at now. I broke down crying because a piece of me died with him. I would not be the leader I was had it not been for his harsh disciplined style demeanor. He was one of the last few leaders in the military who served in the old army and was willing to place his personal feelings about others to the side and place the Army's needs at the forefront. Soaking in the emotion of it all, my desire of revenge kept increasing.

Walking into the chow hall one morning I could see images of New York and other places on TV going crazy like it was New Year's night. "Osama Bin Laden Killed," could be seen flashing across the screen as people celebrated giving hugs and drinking like we had just won the war.

"Now what?" someone asked.

"Now we go on mission. This doesn't change a thing. Some other asshole is just going to take his place. Let's go get the trucks up," I replied.

Pressured with retaliation, the Taliban were determined to kill as many of us as possible for their ol' boy Bin Laden. We all got an awakening as fighting in the Kunar province was increasing. In an instant spark of motivation, my purpose was about to be released. We received orders that our platoon was to reinforce the mountains and push out a major wave of enemy fighters who arrived to the mountains for fighting season.

PFC Doyle, Pech River Valley, 2011

"Fighting is crazy up there, isn't it Sergeant?" PFC Garcia asked.

Garcia was the driver of my truck and his sole purpose was to get us to and from each location safely. The mobility and maneuverability of our team depended on him.

"Yeah, it can be man," I replied.

"Doyle and Melton, start getting our gun up, rearrange the ammunition, and let's find a way to pack more weaponry on this truck. We're going to need it," I said.

PFC Doyle and SPC Melton were my other two soldiers and gun team. They would rotate out of the gun: while one was on the gun, the other prepared ammunition and played an assistant role for the

SPC Melton, Marawara Police Station, 2011

truck during my absence. Doyle was a hotshot with the MK-19 automatic grenade launcher and his precision was one of the best—plus he walked away with the most kills during this deployment.

Melton, who was a more seasoned soldier already had a deployment to Afghanistan under his belt, and was a master with engineering and ensured we had the most combat ready vehicle. He was able to weld a collapsible metal stepping stool directly under the emergency hatch of the vehicle. When you stood on the platform, half of your body was exposed from the roof of the truck and you were greeted with a secondary mounted gun. This meant our truck could have two crew served weapons firing at once. This kept all of us engaged in the fight and made us a single, mobile fighting position. As we pushed north to the mountains, we were to be based out of FOB Joyce. Just to the northwest of us was the Pech River Valley and famous Korengal Valley. I spent all of my time in these valleys during my first deployment—they were known as the Valley of Death. Most of the biggest battles were fought in these mountain ranges. Ten Medal of Honor recipients received recognition for their actions in this treacherous terrains.

It didn't take long for the 2-25 Infantry Battalion, Third Brigade Combat Team, Twenty-fifth Infantry Division, to start using us within their area of operations. Our platoon, much like my first deployment, was split in half into two supersized squads. It wasn't the ideal doctrinal MP way, but it was what worked for us and the environment we were in. Our first week incorporated integration and resupply missions. We customized our trucks to best fit the needs of the mountainous terrain we were now in. An example of this was fully extending a medical litter that we would carry casualties on and hang it on the outside of each truck with a pair of retractable shears that could cut the litter loose. This enabled faster reaction times in the case of a casualty without having

SPC Melton, SPC Garcia, SGT Ambriz, PFC Doyle. Team Zulu, 2012.

to go into the truck and then assemble the litter. SSG Cas also came up with squad standard operating procedures for sensitive items that displayed the serial number and location of the item on each door so that in the event of a rollover or another unit having to utilize our vehicles, one had a general sense of where everything belonged, which kept everything uniform throughout the squad.

I was the only one in the company who had fought in the Kunar province before so I was tasked out as the medic just like my first deployment. Our organic medic was sent home because his wife was having triplets and they did not want him to miss the birth of his children, which I couldn't have agreed more. There's no reason those children needed to grow up without a father and I could've easily covered down as a medic since I was still EMT qualified. I was tasked with another additional duty because I was one of the better shots throughout the squad and I understood how to utilize effective fires in mountainous terrain; I was the designated squad marksman. That meant I would receive an M-14 enhanced battle rifle and conduct missions not only as a team leader and medic, but also as a designated squad marksman. During my off time, I would work hand-in-hand with the reconnaissance platoon who taught me tactical techniques of detection, stocking, target range estimation methods, camouflage, infiltration, special reconnaissance and observation, and target acquisition.

When we trained our local Afghan counterparts, I would take one of my soldiers with me on counter reconnaissance missions against the enemy while utilizing special hiding places within the mountains. For example, at the Marawara Police Station held in outpost 200 meters above the police station. Deep in the dense mountainous terrain the outpost overlooked the Pakistan border and valley beneath. When SSG Cas conducted his talks with a police chief I would infiltrate into the outpost with one of my soldiers. I would be equipped with my sniper rifle and a pack that included additional ammunition, maps, compass, radio, batteries, shooting sock, a basic 72-hour bag of clothes, water, and food. My soldier (Garcia, Melton, and Doyle would rotate), carried an M249 machine gun with a pack that had an additional M4 carbine, ammunition for both weapons systems, and pyrotechnics to include M203 grenades and smoke grenades to conceal our movement if we needed to break contact from the enemy.

Hiking up to an Observation Post above the Marawara Police Station, 2011.

The Marawara Police Station was known for being attacked because of its relative location to the Pakistan border and a Taliban training facility nearby that would train terrorists by attacking the police. We found out quickly this station needed our assistance the most and we were properly tested by the Taliban for entering into their area. The police station was a single building on a hill midway up a mountain face that overlooked a valley and two villages. It was surrounded by World War I type trenches for cover from the inclining mountains around it. No more than 300 meters to the east was the border of Pakistan. One evening, as we stood near the trenches, we talked with the police officers and were killing time after our weekly meeting with the police chief. As I took my helmet off to wipe sweat off my forehead, tracers flew overhead startling me and forcing me to jump into the trench line. With my helmet rolling away from me and my sniper rifle 6 feet away on the barrier, I was completely defenseless. The fire was too effective for any of us to move leaving seven of us pinned down behind the barriers protecting the police station.

"Someone throw me my sniper rifle, I need to move on them!" I yelled.

After my rifle came hurling into the ditch into my lap, I secured my helmet and I was able to get into the fight. I exited the trench and yelled for some of the soldiers to follow me since I knew SSG Cas would be pushing reports on the radio. The problem was with my voice projecting the opposite way and the sound of gunfire, no one followed. Entering the police station, I looked out the side door to try and identify the enemy positions by scanning the ridgelines for any movement. An Afghan police officer ran to my position in the doorway, pointed to the hilltop, and said, "Taliban!" as if I was not aware we were being shot at.

"No shit," I responded.

For whatever reason, this police officer pushed me out of the doorway and into the open for the Taliban to see. I jumped into the ditch for cover and he jumped in after smiling and pointing back at the hilltop and again announcing "Taliban."

"Guy, I know they are there. Now you just showed them where we are!" I shouted.

Just as I said and on cue Taliban machine gun positions hammered the trench I was in. Tracers bit into the dirt around me, which forced me to low crawl forward behind a wall. Acquiring targets with my scope, I used my sniper rifle as a precision firing weapon tried trying to pick off any movement I saw. At other times, when the enemy fire became so effective, I used my rifle as a lone suppressive fire weapon and tried to defend my position at all costs. The sounds of cracking as the bullets broke the sound barrier overhead would not stop. The enemy did an amazing job at having talking guns where they would take turns firing their machine guns and allowing one another to be reloaded with little or no breaks for us to maneuver. SSG Cas had enough of their shit for one day and jumped on the radio to call in support from our soldiers at the trucks below us.

"Doyle, unload on that MK-19 right now. All gunners light those mountains up. Drivers get out of the driver seat and shoot," SSG Cas yelled into the radio.

Without missing a beat and before he could finish his sentence, Doyle acquired his targets and unleashed a barrage of grenades from the MK-19, which was a machine gun that fired belt-fed grenades. *I know, sexy.* I started to see the seriousness of how bad we were suppressed and not being able to move. I could see I needed help and I was running low on ammunition so I grabbed the police officer by the shoulders and tried to send him to get help for us. Without an interpreter, I was talking slow as if that was going to project my point across to him easier.

"Americans. Go get the Americans now. Do you understand me? Get Americans now," I yelled over the gunfire.

He nodded his head, smiled, pointed at the hilltop, and said, "Taliban," and took off. *He's going to screw this up.* SSG Cas, back in his position behind the barriers, had the Afghan police officer run up to his position, looked at him square in the eyes, and instead of saying "American now," he said, "American down." *He screwed it up.*

But what I witnessed later, because it was recovered from SSG Cas helmet video camera was a sight that will forever choke me up. In the video, I saw all six soldiers pinned down; but when they heard I was possibly down, they stood up, disregarded their own safety and came to my rescue. The entire time they were pinned down they were only concerned with returning fire, but because they thought I was wounded, they came to retrieve my body. It was the purest form of brotherhood I could have ever witnessed in combat. I felt so proud to be an American soldier because they lived the ethos of never leaving a fallen comrade behind.

Bemis stuck his head out the window. "Ambriz, are you alive?"

"Yeah man, are you?"

We exchanged laughs and then gunfire. *We made it a date.* This showed me the type of squad we had and the sacrifice we were willing to make for one another. Sometimes it wasn't about brotherhood and sacrifice, other times it was purely luck.

Luck almost landed in our laps two weeks later back at FOB Joyce. My three soldiers and I were standing in line, just outside the chow hall tent for dinner when we were notified SSG Cas wanted to talk to us. We moaned for giving up our spot in line, until four minutes later a rocket landed in the exact spot my team had been standing, peppering shrapnel over other soldiers who had taken our place.

What are the chances? Those poor guys, but I am glad my guys are okay.

Later, I told my team to stay in their rooms and I would sneak out and grab them food so they could eat a hot meal. When I walked outside, the sirens were still going off with not a person outside as they were all located indoors or in the bunkers. I walked into the

SPC Gelinas (left) and SGT Ambriz on a overwatch position, 2011

chow hall for a free buffet full of food all to myself. Score! After I piled the plates full of chicken strips and fries, I headed back to the room, but I didn't get far past the first set of bunkers.

"Hey you, high speed. What the hell are you doing," a random SSG asked me.

"Uh, I had . . . to get chicken strips, Sergeant." I replied.

He chewed my ass for roaming around during the rocket barrage and although it seemed funny at the time, he was right. It was irresponsible, but my mindset was in a different place. I didn't really care about life and death and accepted that whatever happened to me was all a part of the plan. In my mind, if I was a cat, I had gone through all nine lives. I was just waiting for the day I caught that bullet with my face.

The stars started to align and the squad was really starting to sync. Every fluid motion that one person made, the others mirrored and all the pieces seemed to fit perfectly. During night operations, we were always the first activated due to our chemistry and effectiveness. One night, they sent us to respond to an enemy platoon-sized element that was planting yet another IED. We already had six kills under our belts from guys like Burnt Berry trying to plant an IED so it was time to add some tick marks to that number. As we arrived on site the enemy immediately started to disengage from digging and retreat toward the mountains. SSG Cas led a dismounted element toward the enemy fighters and left me to be in charge of our convoy. I was upset at first because I wanted to be on the ground with him and I felt like we weren't going to be able to get in the fight, but boy was I wrong.

As the dismounted element started to move toward the enemy, we could see that the enemy was moving too fast and SSG Cas wasn't going to be able to reach them in time. Doyle—who had become a precision gunner at this point—was able to spot an estimated enemy force of eighteen individuals running perpendicular to our vehicle. Who knew if there were other enemy fighters trying to maneuver on SSG Cas. I had to make a leadership decision. I could not let the enemy get away and I wanted to send a message to anyone else who might be observing our dismounted element.

I'm probably showing my age, but you remember when the original Power Rangers (Mighty Morphin), transformed all of their powers into the Megazord? Well, my truck was about to transform our powers into the Uncle Sam version of Megazord.

SGT Ambriz helping SPC Melton to an observation post.

Everyone in my truck had a key job and we had very little time as every second that went by the enemy got farther away. *"It's Morphin Time!"* Garcia started to maneuver the truck utilizing only his night vision goggles, to a position overlooking the enemy retreat. Doyle and Melton started to feed me information and descriptions of the enemy as well as lacing the target for exact distances. SGT Bemis was an additional person in my truck this day and opened the emergency hatch. With his compass gave me the exact azimuth direction of the enemy from our location. I sent updates to SSG Cas while requesting close air support from rotary wing that was in our area. It was like every individual in that truck knew their job and was proficient enough to feed me information within seconds. I conducted a call for fire with close air support, utilizing the exact distance from Doyle and direction from Bemis while walking in gun runs from our Apache helicopters eliminating all enemy threats before they could retreat.

I have never seen a team so synced and in unison with one another before.

It was the same type of synchronization that we were going to need because the time came to push back the enemy. Back at base, I sat in the briefing room, listening as the plan was set forth: "We're taking back the Pech River Valley and FOB Blessing." FOB Blessing was my first Afghan home when I landed on its doorstep that dark night during my first deployment. Since then the Taliban had seized it. When I left Afghanistan in 2010, the Taliban made a huge push to control the Pech River Valley and now controlled 80 percent of territory we once held. Little did I know the reason they were bringing us back the mountains in the first place was to take back the valley.

I'm going back home where it all started, FOB Blessing. Except this time the enemy isn't going to just give it to us and we are going to have to fight for it. This initiated the Battle for Blessing and Operation Diamond Head.

2nd Platoon, 66th Military Police Pulling security on a police checkpoint roof, fifteen minutes before a close fight with the enemy, 2011.

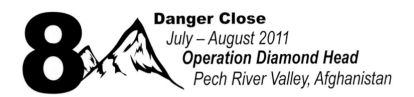

8

Danger Close
July – August 2011
Operation Diamond Head
Pech River Valley, Afghanistan

O ur mission was simple: take back land in the valley, establish strongholds, and flush the enemy out. Coming back to the valley meant bringing humanitarian assistance for the local populace and put bad guys in body bags. *Simple enough.*

Holy shit, I'm back! Talk about déjà vu.

Our MP squad were the first Americans in the valley since the last units retracted earlier that year. As we approached the entrance of the valley, we were to meet with local Afghan police at a checkpoint in order to proceed forward. When we arrived at the checkpoint, smoke had engulfed the building and we found some the police officers beheaded, with their heads on sticks. *God this smell is ripe.* The interpreter said there was a message on the wall from the Taliban.

"What does the message say?" I asked the interpreter.

"Keep coming," he replied.

These assholes are taunting us. Telling us to come deeper into the valley. Wait, this was planned. They have to know we are coming, right? So, how many of them are waiting for us?

Wake up!

For a week, we moved from one stronghold position to another mirroring the infantry, taking pop shots, and being heckled by the enemy. Day four into the operation and we tried to keep ourselves sane since we couldn't leave the trucks for any reason. We conducted our same ritual as the night before, by fighting over and opening all the good MREs. We would drink as many energy drinks as we could, then stay up and talk about every subject imaginable. *Well, time to*

SGT Lane, SGT Ambriz, and SGT Bemis spotting for a sniper in the Pech River Valley, 2011.

pre-game by blessing the energy Gods. We shot gunned three discounted energy drinks each. The sweet nectar that was responsible for fueling military forces through conflicts in the past decade, the well-known Rip It energy drink. Letting the drink hit my bloodline, I closed my eyes and sank my head in the back of my seat.

After about an hour of silence, Garcia and I were eating our dinner in the front seat staring out the windshield into the complete darkness of the Afghan night. From our far right, the huge red ball of an RPG flew directly over our truck and impacted fifteen meters above SGT Lane's truck.

"Sergeant," Garcia asked.

"Yeah man," I replied.

"Was that an RPG?" he asked.

"Yeah man," I replied.

Time to go to work.

As I crawled to the back of the truck, I told Doyle to start utilizing his infrared camera to scan for enemy targets as I opened the emergency hatch and manned the additional crew served weapon on the back of our truck. As I took my headset off to crawl to the back, I told Garcia to start playing some music to really pump me up

120

during this firefight. We had found a way to hotwire our iPod into the internal headset frequencies—*sorry if you're reading this, Cas.*

"I got you, Sergeant." A grin creased his face.

Once through the emergency hatch, with the weapon fully loaded, I grabbed the additional headset in the back so I could communicate with my team on the inside. As soon as I put the headset on and was able to hear the inside of my truck, Taylor Swift could be heard playing throughout our headsets.

"Garcia," I said.

"Yes, Sargento?" he replied in Spanish.

"Screw you."

"Yes, Sargento."

Times like this remind myself how many headaches my soldiers have given me. I know I've aged years because of them but it's been worth it. I've loved every single one of my

PFC Garcia doing a wonderful job pulling security.

soldiers and would do anything for them. I couldn't just say it though. I would need to show it through my actions, display what leadership looked like so that one day, they could carry on that tradition. Every leader has a defining moment that sets a base foundation of one's leadership style allowing the leader to display one's true colors. My defining life moment presented itself during one of the toughest military situations one could be placed in: the enemy surrounding and attempting to overrun you.

On the afternoon of August 4, 2011, we received a call that a humanitarian aid convoy was under attack to the west of us and was in need of immediate assistance. I knew exactly where we were going: the village of Matin (Ma-teen). On my first deployment, we called it the Matin Mile because you would take contact the whole way through the village.

"Alright, listen up guys, the mountains will incline high around us. There is a village close to the road and the vegetation will eat up your flanks so watch your fire when we get in here," I told my soldiers.

We were the third truck of our four-truck convoy so by the time the first truck arrived on scene, we were stopped around the curve of the mountain and couldn't see much. Gunfire could be heard in the distance, but nothing seemed to be aimed at us.

"Power 2-2 (SSG Castellanos), this is Zulu (my callsign), what's going on?" I asked.

"I don't know, but there is a fuel truck blocking the road, an Afghan police officer is wounded, and he's lying in this ditch next to us waving for help," SSG Cas replied.

Shit, we don't have a medic right now and I haven't executed medical duties since my first deployment.

I can't let that police officer bleed out though.

But I don't know the situation or where the enemy is, I could be walking into an ambush.

Screw it.

Wake up.

"Power 2-2, this is Zulu, I am dismounting. I'll grab the wounded."

"Garcia check both radio stations. You're in charge of communications. And get our SATCOM (satellite communication set) up just in case we lose the fill or can't get a hold of anyone. Doyle, start prepping additional rounds and if you get positive identification, start throwing some rounds downrange. Kill these assholes Doyle! Melton, you're in charge of the truck. Make sure these two got everything they need in case I don't come back," I instructed them.

I crawled to the back of the truck and grabbed my small aid bag. I loaded my weapon and told Melton to prep a smoke grenade to conceal my movement. As Melton prepped the grenade and opened the hatch, I took a moment to talk to the Big Guy upstairs. I could tell this was one of those moments that I needed to be selfish and ask God for my forgiveness of sins and get me through this obstacle that lay ahead of me.

"Dear God, hey, it's me again. Sorry I haven't talked to you in a while. I swear if you can get me through this one alive . . ."

Usually during this time, soldiers will swear off their addictions of drinking alcohol or other bad habits in exchange for their life. Begging the Almighty Lord and Savior with our shitty customs deal that will hopefully stray bullets away from us.

Don't kid yourself, you got beer in your fridge right now.

I dropped the ramp once I heard the smoke was out and ran out the back and to the left along the passenger side toward truck one. I looked to my left where the smoke grenade was supposed to be, but it was late on dispersion and I was now completely exposed for the enemy to see. The gunfire got louder the closer I got to truck one. Being the only American outside the trucks, the enemy was taking the opportunity to try and hit me like that carnival duck shooting game. I stopped in front of truck one, looked around to assess my threats, and build a course of action. To my left (driver side of the trucks) was a long stretch of cornfields that led to the base of a mountain that continued up into the clouds. To my right was a small irrigation ditch that inclined up a hill towards a village. About 40 meters in front of me, was an abandoned fuel truck, located perpendicular to the police officer who was lying in the ditch bleeding out. Petitioning for his life and for me to hurry, the police officer cried out in anguish and tried to speak in broken English begging, "Please Soldier, please."

"I'm coming" I said in an annoyed voice similar to my wife telling me to do the dishes.

With little to no suppressive fire support, I sprinted toward the fuel truck, then baseball slid into the ditch straight into a stream of human feces. I crawled my way to the casualty who was panicking and starting to go into shock from slowly bleeding out. Trying to keep myself as small as possible from enemy fire, I reached with my left hand and baseball gripped the police officer's lower leg squeezing as hard as I could to apply pressure to the wound. Reaching with my right hand into my medical equipment pouch I removed a tourniquet and placed it above his bullet wound. After what seemed about three minutes of our position being pounded by the enemy, I knew if I didn't make a move, they would take advantage of it and overrun us. The police officer continued to panic, so I rolled him into my body and hugged him so that my body armor would protect him from any incoming rounds and I would take the bullet instead of him.

Trying not to slide into the small waterway ditch, he curled next to me and dug his nails into my arms holding me as if I were the Savior himself. My left thigh was soaked in his blood from the tourniquet that kept coming undone because he would not stop squirming around. He sporadically tried to dig with his bare hands for more defilade to protect us from incoming fire. The incoming enemy fire was effective; I could hear the smacking of bullets against the wall above my head. My ears were ringing from the explosions and gunfire. Dirt and debris surrounded me as if it were trying to shield me from the enemy. With the police officer screaming his indecipherable language in my right ear, I couldn't understand the traffic on my radio. Then I heard, a loud "Pffftt" sounded behind me. I couldn't pick my head up to look, so I rolled my body backward while keeping my wounded patient close to my body armor. As I looked behind me, I saw what I could only describe as my own Lord and Savior at that moment in time: my squad leader, SSG Castellanos, opened his air compressed door and looked down at me.

"Cas, help! These rounds are getting close and I can't get out of this ditch!" I yelled.

Although I had barely served with Cas, when I looked back at him, he gave me this quiet, yet confident look that set me at ease with all that was going on around me. I didn't even question it I knew he was going to get me out of it alive, so why not go all out.

I rolled back over and looked at the Afghan police officer in the eyes and for the first time he understood perfect English as I told him, "Get ready to run, bitch." He smiled, nodded his head in agreement and

propped himself up to move. Cas pulled his grenade out and threw it not far from the other side of the truck, which I took as my cue to get us out of the kill zone. I grabbed the police officer, threw his arm over my shoulder, and dashed for cover behind the first truck of our four-vehicle convoy. SGT Lane, who was standing on the platform outside his door of truck one, saw five enemy fighters enter the ditch where I had been laying. He grabbed an M249 squad automatic weapon and eliminated all five fighters before they could reach my location. At first, I wondered why Cas threw the grenade so close to the other side of the truck but as I sprinted to SGT Lane's truck for cover, I could see the cornstalks moving heavily as enemy fighters were sprinting toward our location. One of my last vivid thoughts from that moment was, "Jesus Christ, they are going to try and overrun our position."

Then, the thunderous roar from an F-16 came down, as the pilot flew 100 feet off the ground, banked left, and hit his afterburners to conduct a show of force. Everything went deathly silent. I could see the pilot's red helmet, as he was flying so low. LT Pleasants was doing everything he could to get us continued show of force runs. The pilots conducted numerous low fly overs in attempts to keep the enemy back; however, nothing seemed to work. After the back of the truck was opened I carried my patient inside, set him down, and continued to assess him for other injuries while treating his existing ones. His blood oozed onto my left thigh as I lifted his leg to pack gauze into his exit wound and applied a pressure dressing.

"Gelinas (the gunner for truck one I was sitting next to), watch this guy and make sure he doesn't go into shock," I said.

"I'll try but my gun keeps jamming, Sergeant."

Truck one had a mounted gun that was controlled by the gunner from inside the truck so he did not have to be exposed outside to enemy fire. The truck hatch was open as he was sticking his hands out to try and mess with the components to get it to work. By the time I grabbed my weapon and started to recheck my ammo count, the truck got silent. I could hear incoming gunfire from outside, but it was like everything inside got sucked into a seashell; sound was faint, and no one moved. I stopped what I was doing and looked back at Gelinas who was looking up staring at the open hatch to his truck. I peeked my head over and I could not believe what I saw. There he was, 6' 3", 220 lbs of man, SGT Lane, my good friend who served with me on my first deployment. He was kneeling on top of truck one trying to fix the gun. The truck already stood 12-feet tall. With him on the roof above me, he was just a big target exposed in the open with the enemy taking free shots on him.

SGT Ambriz covered in blood. Moments after placing the casualty in the truck and sustaining his wounds.

I watched him completely dazed in amazement. He would take the weapon apart, get shot at. Stop. Pick up his weapon, shoot back, then go back to work on the truck's gun. *This brave son of a bitch. What is he thinking? Well, I can't let him get shot alone. I hope I don't get shot in the face though, I want my family to be able to recognize me.*

126

Wake up!

I threw open the truck's emergency hatch, raised my weapon, and started to acquire targets. *Crack! Crack! Crack! Holy shit, I can't tell where the fire is coming from.* All of a sudden, I felt a tug on my pant leg.

"Sergeant, did you hear?" Gelinas asked.

"No, what?"

"We're surrounded," he said.

"No shit? I couldn't tell. I think they're getting closer though," I said.

Surrounded? Well this isn't the first time I've been surrounded. Few times during my first deployment, but this was different. They were way too close for comfort. Movement was all around us as they were trying to find ways to our trucks through blind spots.

Wake up!

I engaged the enemy to the left, swung right, and engaged up into the village. I did this repeatedly until I went through 500 rounds. I looked over to see Lane pulling off a simple Call of Duty move. He got tired of trying to fix the trigger assembly on the gun, so he yelled down into the truck and told Gelinas to use the camera on the gun to find the enemy to engage. SGT Lane pulled the trigger manually every time Gelinas told him he was on target and, spun around on the roof until I heard him scream.

"Ah, something hit my ass," he yelled.

I assessed his injury and a bullet skimmed his ass cheek. That's when I told him we had enough, we had to get him down, and that this gun was done. Next, we saw SSG Cas run around the truck alone toward the fuel truck blocking the road.

"Come on, we can't let him do this by himself," I said.

I dropped the ramp and ran to the hood of the fuel truck where I started to engage enemy on both sides. I looked over to see SGT Lane grab SSG Cas by the vest and pull him out of the truck.

"You're the squad leader. We need to keep you safe," he yelled.

SGT Lane threw his weapon in the fuel truck and dropped the keys on the floor; as he bent over to grab the keys, enemy bullets penetrated the windshield where Lane's head had been. He quickly threw the truck into reverse, rammed it into the ditch, and emptied the fuel so the Taliban could not capture it and utilize its resources.

The local commander told us he was sending an Infantry unit to replace us, but until they got there, we had to sustain the causality and defend our positions against the enemy at all costs.

Okay, time to go to work.

Wake up!

SSG Cas, SGT Lane, and I stood our ground to cover the flanks of our vehicles from dismounted enemy fighters who were using the cornfields as concealment to maneuver and get closer.

"Lane, they are getting close man! You got a boom box? We need some grenades to keep them back," I yelled.

SGT Lane and SGT Ambriz

I grabbed as many M203 rounds (grenades that can be shot from the grenade launcher attached to my rifle) that I could find and started to fire them in a pattern in the cornfield hitting their egress routes. I fired so many grenades that my launcher detached from my rifle and my weapon became disabled and ineffective to use. I threw my weapon into truck one and told the driver to give me his M249—a squad automatic weapon that weighs roughly 22 pounds (with a 200-round drum) and can fire up to 850 rounds a minute. As I loaded my M249 ammunition onto the feed tray, I looked around to see targets as they maneuvered around us. It was hard to see with the debris and smoke filling the area, but I saw their shadows moving in the cornfield. They were coming for us.

I could hear the Taliban yelling at one another formulating plans to get around us. It gave me chills down my spine to hear them that close. I could tell they were trying to get close enough so we couldn't use our grenades. The battle was coming down to sheer will, of who wanted it more. They wanted to completely annihilate us in place, take over our trucks, and drag us through the village; however, that shit just wasn't going to happen.

"Lane, they are getting closer! Look at the cornstalks. They're about 22 meters away!" I yelled.

"Give me that flashbang," Lane demanded.

"Why?"

"I just want to scare the shit out of them. I don't care at this point." He giggled.

I grabbed my M249, racked my first round in, took a deep breath, and headed to the back of truck one. It was then that I was about to experience one of the scariest moments of my life.

Ok, Lane is at the front of the truck. I just need to cover the rear, watch these paths, and make sure they don't get an RPG off.

Wait, what is SGT Buyno waving at?

I looked into the windshield of truck two to see SGT Buyno waving his hands hysterically, but I couldn't tell what he was trying to say. Whatever. I raised my weapon, placed the buttstock in my shoulder, and circled around the back of the truck facing the cornfields to the south.

Simultaneously, my eyes focused, my breath was taken from me, and my heart stopped. This can't be.

Hurry, wake up!

In slow motion, three Taliban fighters exited the cornfield no more than 8 feet in front of me. All four of us were shocked to see one another. Time stopped, but the battle raged on outside our glass bubble. All three of the Taliban fighters' eyes opened wide, they yelled to one another, and then started to raise their weapons at me.

Shit! They are so close! Where did they come from?

They are still running toward me. Do I go hand to hand?

I guess this is how I die.

Hurry, do something! Wake up!

Using my weapon as a paint brush, my canvas was their bodies. I aimed at the far-right enemy fighter and while holding down the trigger, I traced the muzzle of my weapon from the right as the recoil lifted it to the left. Holding my breath, I watched as my bullets cut the enemy fighters in half. From torso to heads, pink mist blood splattered and skulls of the enemy imploded as their bodies fell at the base of the cornfield. I retraced my weapon and saw their limp bodies roll off the side of the road. Moaning and grunting from their last breaths could be heard as their souls left their bodies. I retreated to the back of the truck and started to reload my weapon and catch my breath.

"Lane, Cas, they are about to overrun us," I yelled.

Sitting behind the tire, I peeked my head back around the truck to make sure there was not a second wave of fighters coming in when I noticed one of the fighters I shot was partially lying on the road and was trying to crawl back into the cornfield. I could have easily swung back around the truck, put him out of his misery, and shot him in the head. But I didn't. Instead, We both locked eyes as he was too weak to pull himself anymore.

It was like we both stopped what we were doing and took a moment of peace from the whole thing. Two men embracing a moment, fighting for what they believed in. His moment came to a halt however as his body went limp and his dead weight rolled back into the cornfield.

We started to grab all the hand grenades we had. While using direct fire against the village, we rolled grenades into the cornfield to keep the dismounted fighters back. Engaging both sides with little cover, we kept traversing and reengaging targets until we became overwhelmed. My weapon was running dry and it needed lubricant to keep it going but that was back in my truck over 75 meters away.

Well, I'm getting my workout today.

I sprinted with my M249 back to my truck and entered through the rear ramp. As the ramp was closing, it caught my foot, smashing it. I screamed and Melton disengaged the ramp and freed my foot.

"God, that hurt, I can't feel my foot. Give me the CLP (weapon lubrication). I need to lube these guns." I said.

"Roger, here Sergeant. Is everything okay? Can I come out and help?" Melton asked.

"No, stay here. These guys need you. I don't need you getting killed. Open the ramp. I'm going back."

You know, years later, I look back and I feel like that was a very selfish moment of me. I knew it was dangerous and maybe I made the right tactical call, but, a part of me wonders if I took experience away from my soldiers getting in the fight. I just wanted to be selfish because I did not want to have to drag my soldiers home like I did LT Parten. I refused to put my soldiers in a body bag.

SGT Ambriz, clearing cornfields, Pech River Valley, 2011

"Sergeant… Sergeant, Wake up!"

"Sergeant!" Garcia yelled.

"What?" I replied as I stopped and turned around.

Kneeling in the back of the truck, I looked up to see all three of my soldiers sitting in silence not engaging the enemy or spotting enemy positions. They were just staring at me like they were about to break some bad news to me. I could hear bullets smacking the side of our truck and mumbled words from the cracking radio in the background.

"Air support just radioed in. They believe we're surrounded by an enemy force of 150 fighters," Garcia said.

"Yeah, it feels like it." I gave him a dead stare.

"Hey Sarge. There's sixteen of us. We're kind of outnumbered," he said.

All three of my soldiers sat there, quiet, staring at me for an answer and guidance. I thought about what my NCOs would have said to me. I thought about that day back in September when I was the nervous Private. I tried to replicate my NCOs and their demeanor. So, I gave them a smile and put my hand on Doyle's shoulder.

"That just means there's more targets for us to hit, start knocking them down, get me some kills. Tell LT to get us some more close air support. We're gonna need it," I smirked.

I could tell I was giving Garcia a stare like I would never see him again. I slapped Doyle's face in a love tap manner for good luck. Then, I brought my eyes to Melton and gave him a look like entrusting him with my children.

"Melton, take care of them. I have to get back out there. Now drop the ramp."

Combat is brutal and harsh and requires men to be just as brutal in order to succeed. In that moment, my soldiers knew I needed them to dig in and revert to their primal stages to overcome the enemy.

As I ran back to truck one, they told me they were going to push up the road, turn around, and prepare for our replacement unit to arrive in fifteen minutes. As I got into truck one, I figured I would get into the fight since the gun was still down. I climbed up and exposed my upper body and engaged targets on both sides. Because my radio died, I had no way to hear communications. The F-16 announced he was coming in for a danger close strafing run—normally depending on the size of the rounds and type, 200 meters is considered extremely danger close. He would be performing hits at 25 meters from our trucks. The pilot decided to utilize his 20mm six-barrel Gatling gun, which fires at 6,000 shots per minute. As he came in for his gun run, dirt and debris were kicked up from the cornfield massacre he was distributing on them and raining down on me and the top of the truck.

Jesus that was close! I can't hear shit.

God, I'm tired.

Wait, what is that to the left?

Wake up!

Above me and to the left in the village an enemy fighter appeared around the corner of a building. As he swung his AK-47 around and toward me, he fired multiple times at me hitting the top of the truck. With my unfocused eyes, I raised my weapon and acquired my target with the buttstock of my rifle barely on my cheek and fired three shots into his upper torso. Before I could see what happened to him, something snapped my head back and stung my face one inch below my left eye. I collapsed into the truck and fell into SGT Lane's lap. The hot barrel of my gun landed on a case of Monster energy drinks exploding half of them all over inside the truck.

"Lane, I think I'm hit. My face hurts," I said.

"Zulu is hit. I say again Zulu is hit." Lane announced over the radio.

All I could think about were my soldiers in that truck alone hearing on the radio I was hit.

They probably think I'm dead.

I felt like I was letting them down.

"It's just a small piece of shrapnel. You're fine." He pulled the small piece of metal out of my face and threw it on the floor.

"Ow! Asshole. Oh yeah, sorry about the monsters by the way." I said.

As we laughed, we both looked out the front windshield only to witness one of the most badass American sights you could see. SSG Cas was running along the cornfield to the rear of our convoy to link up with the Infantry unit replacing us. While running, he was engaging targets. When his weapon finally ran out of ammunition, an enemy fighter appeared out of the corn stalks. It was just him versus Cas and we could do nothing but watch. Without hesitation Cas dropped, slung his M4 rifle, drew his M9 pistol, acquired his target, and eliminated the threat with two shots to the chest as he kept running.

"Ambriz, what the hell did we just see?" Lane asked.

"I don't know man. I have blood in my eye. I can't see shit. But I think I just saw Cas kill someone with a pistol, right?" I asked.

"Right." Lane replied.

"Right... well, I'm going to go sit down now. I'm tired." I said.

I can't believe I just witnessed Cas kill this guy with a pistol. I'm forever dubbing him the name Pistol Pete.

SSG Castellanos, AKA Pistol Pete

Once Cas reached the rear of our convoy, he linked up with our replacement unit, explained to them the situation, and pointed out the enemy positions. After we were relieved from the area, we received clearance to head back to base and refit.

Sitting in the back of truck one, I took my helmet off, rubbed the blood off my face, and tried to decompress what had just happened. These mountains sure do know how to leave grueling scars on you; they never seem to disappoint. The fighting was so intense it took every ounce of energy from me.

"You okay, Sergeant?" Gelinas asked.

"I'm fine. I just need a second."

Get yourself together Ambriz. Soldiers are looking at you. Pick your head up and stop feeling sorry for yourself. You're still alive.

Do not show them this emotion.

After we headed back to base, we dropped the casualty off at the aid station, cleaned the brass out of our truck, washed the blood off, refit all of our ammunition, and headed right back out into sector. This went on for another week or so until we finally seized FOB Blessing and the remainder of the Pech River Valley back from the Taliban.

A few weeks later I was walking back from chow, I was stopped by my lieutenant.

"Ambriz, you guys did good out there," he said.

"Thank you, Sir."

Not knowing which words to choose, he looked down awkwardly as he took a deep breath and returned his gaze to my eyes.

"We put you in for another Bronze Star with Valor." He placed his hand on my chest and then walked away.

I stood there speechless. The same emotions from my first deployment came rushing back. I didn't know what to say or think as I was not prepared for the scrutiny and spotlight again that came with that award. A single tear came down my face as I looked at the sunset crest the mountain pass.

Hey LT Parten, can you believe this shit-show?

I can't believe I've made it this far. I wish you were still here though. I could use your guitar playing to calm me down. I don't know how much more my soul can take with this valley. I feel like the mountains' shadows are pulling me into hell. Well, here's to the next eight months left in this deployment.

Wake up!

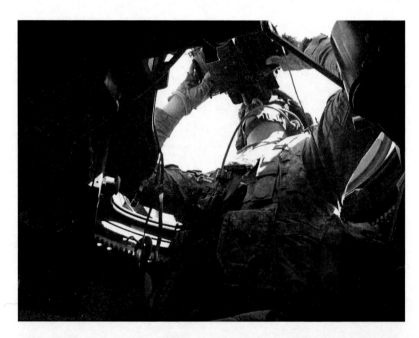

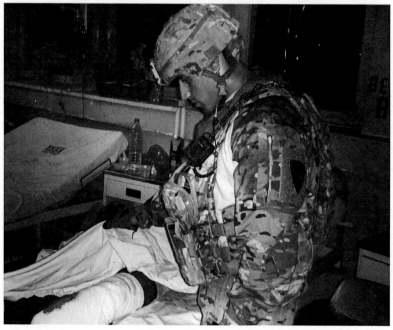

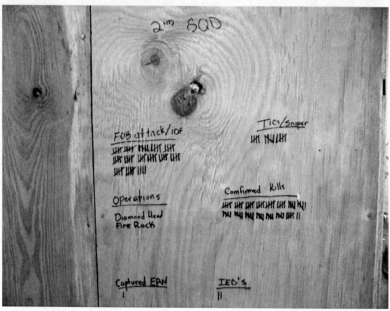

9 The Aftermath
April 2012 – Current
Fort Leonard Wood, Missouri

"Attention to orders!"

"To all who shall see these presents, greeting: This is to certify that the President of the United States of America authorized by executive order, 24 August 1962 has been awarded the Bronze Star Medal with Valor device to Sergeant Sean T. Ambriz. For valorous actions and meritorious actions while engaged in direct combat operations in support of Operation Enduring Freedom on 4 August 2011. Sergeant Ambriz' courage and selfless dedication in a combat zone, under the most extreme circumstances, greatly contributed to the fight against the war on terrorism. Sergeant Ambriz' actions reflect great credit upon himself, Task Force Peacekeeper, Combined Joint Task Force-1 and the United States Central Command. Signed, Daniel B. Allyn, Major General, US Army, Commanding.

It all feels different this time. I'm older. I'm wiser. I think?

This burden feels a bit heavier now, but it's a pain I'm used to. I understand the responsibility this place has on me as a representation of the military police corps, but do I have the mental fortitude for this? I guess I don't have a choice.

Wake up!

"So, I hear you have two of these Bronze Stars now, both with Valor devices, so what does that mean?" Major General Anderson asked.

"Yes sir, I guess I am very lucky," I stared straight ahead.

"That's a lot of responsibility you know."

"Thanks for the pressure Sir."

SSG Cas, SGT Ambriz, LT Pleasants. PFC Doyle, and PFC Layne also pictured to right received the Army Commendation Award with Valor.

"I don't think there's any pressure you can't handle," he said as he imitated the same motions my battalion commander did, almost exactly two years prior, pulling on my uniform collar and pinning on me a second Bronze Star with Valor.

As I walked off the stage to my right, I took a seat and stared into the distance of my own black hole for the remainder of the ceremony. After it was complete, I stood outside in the hallway shaking the hands of every individual who attended the ceremony welcoming their congratulatory comments with my repetitive thank you's, even though I felt dead and out of place at that moment. Don't get me wrong, it felt amazing to be home this time around, maybe because I had my wife this time as opposed to my first deployment when I came home to an empty barracks room. But I couldn't help but wonder why I still felt so empty.

Being back home the second time around seemed a lot harder than the first as I couldn't even function doing daily activities. You would think with my experience of understanding the emotions and having a more supporting cast behind me I could prevail past these situations, but I couldn't. I found myself afraid of things that I shouldn't have been afraid of, but it's what they resembled that scared the shit out of me. I couldn't drive my car near tall grass or vegetation that resembled cornfields without freaking out. Driving by my first set of tall grass, I found myself sinking into my seat absolutely convinced Taliban were going to run out and overrun my position. The grass was too tall, the wind blew it too fast, and I couldn't tell where the movements were coming from. *Shit, what's in there?* I couldn't quite explain what was wrong, but I was far more scared than I'd ever been in Afghanistan, probably because I had no way of defending myself at this point and I didn't have friends like Lane or Cas over watching my position. I didn't think that what I was experiencing had anything to do with combat; I just thought I was going crazy.

After two weeks home, I had my first real, "this is serious" moment during a night of sleep with my wife. Aimee likes to sleep with the covers over her head, and I still had problems of waking up throughout the night and checking my surrounding areas. I was having a nightmare replaying the Battle for Blessing. Where I woke up to see what looked like a Taliban member with his head wrapped near me. I instantly was thrown back into the moment defending those cornfields so I did the only thing I knew and tried to eliminate the threat. I started to choke my wife, but thankfully I snapped out of it within seconds and realized what was actually happening. I couldn't believe that it had gotten to that point, which instantly sparked my anxiety. See the good thing about anxiety is it always keeps you ready in the fight by staying aware and on your toes. The problem was there was no more fight to be fought, except the one in my own head.

No one talks to yourself more in a day than yourself and my head wouldn't shut the hell up.

I found myself having a harder time trying to wrap my head around my own thoughts and actions. It was as if the valley's shadows that once covered me were now in between my two ears. The valley controlled all of my thoughts and actions and I had little say in the matter. Regardless of where I went, the distinctive attributes of the valley followed me and reminded me of it. I knew I needed to cleanse my body with some type of purification I felt riddled with toxic, which was going to eat at me if I didn't get help. The only help I wanted was from the dead and if you listen closely, the dead do talk. I was seeing LT Parten everywhere I went; I even grabbed a man in the grocery store one day thinking it was him and I somehow was in a bad dream.

See, what no one ever tells you is that going to war is hard but sometimes the hardest part about going to war is coming home.

By my second month home, I stayed indoors and I didn't want to go anywhere or see anyone. As I was taking my dog for a walk one evening, I looked off into the distance and just to the right of Cheyenne Mountain was a huge fire that got swept by the wind and hurled downward toward the city of Colorado Springs. I immediately knew by the size of this fire it was going to be devastating so I jumped into my truck and grabbed my aid bag and drove straight toward the fire. By the time I got to the biggest intersection near the fire, the police department already had the area cordoned off. As I pulled up to the police officer, I showed him my aid bag and told him I was an EMT and that I was there to help. He told me I could not drive into the, area but if I wanted to run, and that I was looking at anywhere between 5 and 7 miles to the nearest fire. Once I parked my truck, I grabbed my aid bag and I called my platoon sergeant, SFC Waterhouse, to let him know he was probably going to get in trouble because of my actions. While running, I sent him a small brief of the situation and of what I was doing. Although he knew he was also going to get his ass chewed, he told me to be careful and save whoever I could.

What an adrenaline rush, not like combat, but it's the first thing in two months that makes me feel alive again.

About four miles into my run, I met up with two Colorado Springs detectives who saw me running toward the fire and tried to evacuate me before I told them I was there for the same reason. They needed all the hands they could get with a lot of area to cover. Since the majority of the senior citizens and other residents had no idea the fire was heading their way. We went door-to-door rescuing whoever we could extract from the area. After it was all said and done, we extracted dozens of individuals from their homes no more than 100 feet from the fire. After almost two weeks of work, the fire left two people dead, 346 homes and 18247 acres burned. A week later, my command sergeant major congratulated me with the Military Outstanding Volunteer Service Medal.

I could see it on all of their faces at the ceremony. "What a medal chaser", they probably thought. I wanted to take my medals and shove it up their stupid asses, but I guess that's not the professional thing to do. Above it all, these people looking at me and talking about me. They had no idea about the internal struggles I currently had. I was tired of the scrutiny and the telephone game talks behind my back. I just wanted to serve. I just wanted to be a part of something bigger than myself. I just wanted to feel like that douche on all the Army commercials with that recruiting song. *Makes you want to join every time.* I wanted to feel bigger than these awards. I wanted others to look at me and understand how I earned them and not think that I was where I was only because of them.

I started acting out at work and one of my mentors pulled me aside to discuss the issues I was having with these awards. He was a Desert Storm veteran who was dodging scud missiles when I was just a baby shitting myself. I told him how I was feeling and how I was so frustrated with how people perceived me and these awards. He grabbed me by the shoulders and sternly told me to shut the hell up, man up, and understand what I was representing. He told me not a lot of military police are placed in a situation where I was. Not many military police served as a medic and squad marksman. A smaller fraction of that has earned the awards that I have earned and those that did earn theirs', not all made it back home alive. So, when I'm bitching about receiving those awards, I am doing nothing but shitting on the graves of better soldiers than myself who earned the same award. He told me I needed to understand it was bigger than myself.

It was then I made the conscious decision to not be silent about my feelings and thoughts. It was also my responsibility to be a steward of the awards. I also made the choice to put my soldiers first and use my experiences to their advantage. Thanks to my mentor, he established a huge chunk of what is now my leadership style. I needed to represent the MP Corps to my fullest ability, because at a minimum it is what I owed the corps.

He could not have been further from the truth.

As time has gone on, it was not just my mental aspect that had been breaking down, but my spiritual and physical as well. When I first joined the Army, a chaplain was handing out Bibles and since there wasn't much to do during downtime in basic training, I used to read it because being a Catholic it was deeply rooted in me to have a strong faith. I carried that Bible in my pocket with me to my first unit and through my entire first deployment. When I got home from that first deployment, that Bible wasn't carried so much anymore and by my second, it didn't even go with me. I still have it wrapped up in the same Ziploc bag I placed it in eleven years ago. It is still unopened, just like my faith. Now I'm not saying I don't believe in God or a higher power anymore, but some of the things that happened in Afghanistan strayed me away from my faith. I wanted to reconnect over the years, but my mental and physical aspect seemed to have taken priority since those have been collapsing so much. I guess if I can't get my head out of my ass and reconnect with my faith sometime soon when I'm standing before the Man I'll have to answer for my sins and hopefully He can forgive me.

I've been pretty lucky over the years because my wife has been amazing through this process even though I haven't always given her a reason to and I haven't always been the best husband. But I'm working on it, I promise. She has always tried to find ways to support me and not get frustrated with my TBI and PTSD. My family has always been supportive, and I have had some good friends that allow me to vent to them so overall, I've been a pretty lucky individual. The sad thing is there are not as many lucky people out there that have that same support system that I do. I try my best and be that extra support for anybody that needs it, but not everybody is as willing to be open about their experiences as I am. Sometimes, it takes a good leader to recognize when people need help. And that's the best thing about being an NCO, you can be a twenty-one-year-old, pin on sergeant, and the Army expects you to have a master's degree in psychology, sociology, and human resources. That is the advantage of being such

a young leader in today's modern Army because there is also a human dimension that has to be factored in on decisions and if a leader cannot recognize these, he's going to fail his or her soldiers. The difficulty I have had is that I have been trying to take care of soldiers long before I tried to take care of myself.

Traumatic brain injury has rattled my memory and thought process as the years have gone on. My

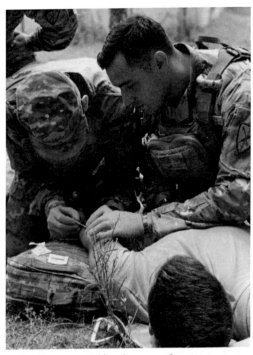

Teaching young Soldiers how to perform intravenous therapy, Joint Base Lewis- McChord, 2018.

shoulder still has problems to this day even though I've tried steroidal injections, surgery, and other forms of rehabilitation. It's slowly giving out. My lower back has collapsed on me twice, which has now affected my hips with one hip flexor being torn and my alignment being thrown off. I have lost 1/2 inch in height with my spine being compressed from wearing gear so much and taking the incline of those mountains day in and day out. Both my knees have given out recently as I've been writing this book and I have put running on hold for a little bit while I do physical therapy for a torn ACL. Finally, my right ankle with one surgery under his belt has lost twenty percent of its flexibility and is getting worse. Pain in my body is a constant reminder of what it was for. Every morning I wake up cracking certain joints and ligaments during my first couple steps just to lube up my body— reminding me for the rest of my life what the sacrifices were for.

What a beautiful burden.

When people thank military members for their sacrifice, they are referring to the deployments and field cycles for extended periods of time away from loved ones. In my mind, the sacrifice is the mental and physical deterioration of one's overall health, because there's no returning from that. Over the years, I've tried everything I could to regain some type of mental strength and I go to the gym every day to try and replicate my twenty-one-year-old self even though I know that neither are attainable.

So, what now?

I haven't deployed since 2012 and the past seven years have been a rebuilding stage for me—but I haven't gotten very far. I've grown in age and matured in some ways, but the only thing that has kept me going is my purpose. To a soldier, the purpose is "The why?" Why am I doing this? Why am I here? Soldiers ask questions all of the time and without purpose it gives them no drive or motivation. The reason I haven't written this book sooner was because after my deployments I found myself taking jobs with higher levels of responsibility. I served as a squad leader, special reaction team NCO, and platoon sergeant. All three jobs have consumed the past seven years of my life and have been keeping me busy. The most important thing about all of those jobs and the only thing that has kept me going and not turn to suicide, has been my soldiers. I have been downright blessed to have some of the best soldiers the MP Corps could produce. I don't know if it's fate or luck, but I have been truly blessed and there's not a day that goes by that I don't think about all of my past soldiers. So, to me that was my purpose. My purpose was to spread my experience and knowledge from my deployments to the younger generation just as my NCOs did when they got back from Iraq and I got to my first unit

At times in the past, I let my purpose get the best of me by occasionally placing my job first and my wife second. When your country puts so much responsibility and the weight of other lives on your shoulders on a daily basis, it can take a nasty toll on you. The problem I have noticed is that we are amazing at taking care of soldiers, but we suck at taking care of our leaders. Our leaders are human too.

The issue now is that PTSD seems to find ways to evolve around your life in particular situations. Earlier last year when I completed my platoon sergeant duties, I also completed a major stage in my career that usually ends in the death of some of us. Any position the Army gives me from this point forward, I will no longer be in the in direct presence of soldiers but more of an administrative role, working hand-in-hand with a commander being the senior enlisted advisor and no longer kicking in doors and shooting the shit with soldiers.

The reason I enlisted—for the days of brotherhood—have come to an end and it is the end of an era I am not willing to let go. Currently, I no longer have soldiers as I am an instructor for the Military Police Senior Leader Course. Although it's a very rewarding job and I'm glad that I was selected, I no longer

SFC Ambriz during ruck march with his platoon, JBLM, 2018

sit with my purpose. I teach in a classroom setting and I no longer have any field rotations leaving me to feel like anything but a soldier. I have a lot more time on my hands for personal improvements, but with time comes thinking and when you think too much, it can lead you down a dark road.

If there is one thing I have learned as a leader, it is that you don't have to have taken a life, seen a life taken, or dragged a corpse across the battlefield to have PTSD. At times I think PTSD is more about recurring fear and the inability to shake it. Fear has a way to shape us create in us a sharper, clearer violence of action. But that shaping of our personality, is permanent. The more fear we experience, the more we are changed.

There are moments we carry with us as we go through life. For me they are the moments outlined in this book. Others have different moments. My old leader used to tell me he can remember the birth of his kids, and the marriage to his wife; but the clearest memory he has is from combat.

For every mission, there is a moment where you transition from the relative safety of the base you are on into the combat zone. In that moment everything was clear from the smell of gas from the truck to the heat from sunlight on your face, to the distinct smell of CLP

2nd Platoon, 66th Military Police Company. My time as a Platoon Sergeant. Joint Base Lewis- McChord, WA 2017.

(weapon lubrication) from the weapons. Calling in the departure report was like signing into a fight. I took inventory of each soldier, in the off chance it might be the last time and checked his own weapon in case it was the only thing that stood between him and the enemy. Every other event from the deployment was like a movie out of focus like the old VHS before the tracking adjustments kicked in. Every departure every time I crossed that invisible line between safe and combat, I can remember that as if I had just conducted the last mission the day before.

Fear drives us, but it creates the warrior for battle. Our minds call to us to wake up in peacetime to create in us the capability to come home. There is no magic pill for PTSD, no magic counseling session, and no magic relationship to fill the gap. In my case, the vacuum left by the battles was a lot more than I realized it would be.

I'm no psychologist and the only thing I can figure is that I still have more to do. The beauty of the Army is that you never know when a story, or a memory creates a butterfly effect in a soldier that could save their life. Maybe it makes them more careful or it's just

enough to remind them to CLP a weapon so it doesn't seize up. Or maybe it's enough to teach a soldier to look left just in time to see an enemy. We never know when our guidance really impacts our troops. I will always remember my time in the valley. I will always remember

Left to Right: Kevin Wood, Jon Denton-Aisner, Eric Dugan, Sean Ambriz, Christopher Mendes attending Justin Riling's funeral, 2019.

those who didn't make it back. Just the same those memories are what I use to fuel me forward.

My body might be failing—hell, my mind might be failing—but there is still one thing I know I can be sure of. I have a responsibility to share my story with my soldiers to create an awareness that they receive without having to go through what I did. I have an additional responsibility to the civilians that support us so that they can better understand their countrymen who return from war. I have a responsibility to my wife to take every step available to become better for her. In the end, it is my choice to move forward in my peace-time self. Until my name is called again to go to the fight, I will continue to fight at home to help myself, and to help my brothers and sisters heal from battle.

Wake up, wake up, wake up!

I've been telling myself to wake up for a long time now. Key moments have come across and I've had to try to snap out of it, yet nothing seems to work. I keep having the same dream where I am standing in the valley surrounded by Taliban, but no one is moving. The enemy looks down upon me and I stand there looking down at a casket. Inside the casket is a younger version of me, PFC Ambriz. Looking at the enemy and back down at standing behind the casket is LT Parten, SGT Powell, and SPC Mace. Everyone including myself looks faded, almost ghostly. No matter how hard I try, I cannot find a way out of that casket or that valley. A part of me will forever roam that valley as a ghost, never out of the fight.

But make no mistake-even if I heal in peace, if my country calls my name, I will not be returning alone. When I cross that invisible line and I sign into that battle, I will be bringing my ghosts from the valley with me and we will begin that age old battle of good and evil until I am no longer needed or no longer capable.

REST IN PEACE

1LT Tyler E. Parten

SGT Joshua D. Powell

SGT Justin Riling

SGT Andrew Schaffer

SGT Zachary Richmond

SPC Stephan Mace

"We will not be intimidated. We will not back down. We've seen war. We don't want war. But if you want war with the United States of America there is one thing I can promise you so help me God. Someone else will raise your sons and daughters."

—Medal of Honor recipient, former SSG David Bellavia

10

Resources

"You don't need a reason to help people."

I understand that not everybody has been forwarded the same opportunities that I have had. That being said I recognize there are those out there wearing the same uniform but are having it a hell of a lot worse than I am. Others a sacrificed more, others have endured more, and others have way less of a support system. I want to make sure that there are resources available for those who are in

need. I just want every veteran to know that they are not alone and there's always somebody there willing to help you.

Leaders, understand people are not robots and there is always a human dimension to every decision we make. Utilize these resources and always place the soldiers first. Without the soldiers the mission will never get done. Even if they do not have social media or the Internet to gather information if they pick up this book, they are able to get the help they need. Finally, I would also like to take this opportunity to present a beautiful foundation that was established, the 1LT Tyler Parten Memorial Fund.

1LT Tyler Parten Foundation

"It gives us some peace knowing Tyler's spirit lives on through the works of others. With your support, his memory will live on and continue to improve the lives of children all over the world. We would like to thank those who have previously donated and continue to keep his memory alive."

While in Afghanistan, shortly before his death in September 2009, Tyler wrote to his family in an email, "Many of my missions revolve around civil affairs; bringing projects like running water and electricity to places that have never had such luxuries. While doing the assessments, I get to interact with the locals and otherwise try to put a friendly face to the American name. I've had many opportunities to interact with the children, whom I believe are the future of this country, so I always to take the time to show them a little affection. I can't tell you how much of a blessing these opportunities are. I'm convinced that if we can win their hearts and improve their lives, maybe it'll all be worth it."

You can make your donation online through West Point at:

https://secure.west-point.org/tylerparten/memorial/

or mail to:

1st Lt Tyler Parten Memorial Fund

C/O ARCF

1400 W. Markham, suite 206

Little Rock, AR 72201

The mission of the Military Police Regimental Association is to promote the history and preserve the traditions of the Military Police Corps Regiment while supporting Military Police Leadership, Soldiers and Families Army wide.

14296 South Dakota Ave
Fort Leonard Wood, MO 65473
Phone: 573-329-6772 / Gift Shop: 573-329-5317

About the MPRA

Through various programs and events, the MPRA is able to provide opportunities for their members and communities. From helping Soldiers and their families in need to providing scholarships, there's something for everyone to participate in. Donations for the various programs are greatly appreciated.

SCHOLARSHIP PROGRAM

The Scholarship Program awards scholarships annually to children and spouses of standard MPRA members. Students may be enrolled, or planning to enroll, in an accredited college or university in a program of undergraduate and graduate studies. The program was established in 2006 with the purpose of providing educational tools to the family members of the Military Police Corps Regiment. We have awarded $276,800 to 295 family members to continue their educational goals to date. The MPRA Scholarship Program is made possible through generous contributions from friends of the MPRA and from proceeds from a variety of fundraising efforts.

BENEVOLENT FUND PROGRAM

The MPRA Benevolent Fund is dedicated to provide financial relief to members and retirees of the Military Police Corps Regiment and Soldiers or civilians working in support of the Military Police Corps Regiment in times of need. Established in 2007, the MPRA is proud of the fact that over $150,000 has been distributed to date. Membership is not a requirement to benefit from this program but it is strongly encouraged. Leaders at all levels are encouraged to take advantage of the fund whenever they have exhausted all means to financially support Soldiers and family members in times of need. The Benevolent Fund is one of the many ways that the MPRA supports Soldiers around the world every day.

MILITARY POLICE MEMORIAL GROVE and REGIMENTAL WALKWAY

The Military Police Regimental Walkway and Memorial Grove has come a long way over the years. You can visit the Grove just about any time of the day and you will see people of all ages paying homage to our Regiment's heroes as well as all MP's past, present and future. The Memorial Grove contains 3 statues that are significant to the Regiment. The first is a bronze crossed pistol archway that has become known as the "Gateway to the Regiment." The second is a 10-foot high bronze replica of the World War II era MP Soldier who is directing traffic on the battlefield in the "Of the Troops and For the Troops" art piece. The third is the Marechaussee on Horseback overlooking Memorial Grove. Two additional walls for the units to dedicate plaques and a bridge over a historical marker leads to the completed foundation for the walkway. Lights were installed throughout the Grove which now allows for visits after dark. Dedicated granite benches and trees display the names of Soldiers who have paid the ultimate sacrifice and MP Units around the world. Thousands of bricks line the walkway that honor individual Soldiers as well as units. The Regimental Walkway is truly an amazing and awe inspiring place to visit.

To make a donation please visit:
https://www.mpraonline.org/shop/legacy-donation/

U.S. Army Soldier and Family Resources

Urgent Needs Phone Numbers

Veteran in crisis line: 1-800-273-8255 or Send a text to 838255

Suicide Prevention Lifeline: 1-800-273-8255

NVF Lifeline for Vets: 1-888-777-4443

VA Suicide Hotline: 1-800-273-8255

National Suicide Hotline: 1-800-273-TALK (8255)

Stop Soldier Suicide: 1.800.273.8255 #1

Military One Source: 800-342-9647

Sexual Assault Safe Helpline: 877-995-5247

Moving and Housing

Post Location Tool: Search every U.S. Army Garrison and their individual information and contact numbers. https://home.army.mil/imcom/index.php/garrisons

Off-post Military Housing

HOMES.mil is a service designed to connect Service members and their Families with community housing rental listings located near U.S. military bases. Type in your current or future installation above to begin searching for homes or create an account to take advantage of HOMES.mil account features or to list your own rental property. Property Managers can list their properties at no cost.
https://www.homes.mil

Passport Services

Phone: 1-877-487-2778/ 1-888-874-7793 (TDD/TTY)
Customer service representatives are available:
Monday–Friday, 8:00 a.m. to 10:00 p.m. Eastern Time
Saturday, 10:00 a.m. to 3:00 p.m. Eastern Time
*Except on Federal Holidays
Automated passport information is available 24 hours a day, 7 days a week.

Department of Defense schools

DoDEA, as one of only two Federally-operated school systems, is responsible for planning, directing, coordinating, and managing prekindergarten through 12th grade educational programs on behalf of the Department of Defense (DoD). DoDEA is globally positioned, operating 163 accredited schools in 8 districts located in 11 foreign countries, 7 states, Guam, and Puerto Rico.
https://www.dodea.edu/

Communities (Army MWR)

G9 integrates and delivers Family and Morale, Welfare and Recreation programs and services enabling readiness and resilience for a globally-responsive Army.
https://www.armymwr.com/

US Department of Veterans Affairs National Center for PTSD

Post-Traumatic Stress Disorder

- USA Cares pays essential household bills while a wounded service member or veteran is attending residential treatment for traumatic brain injury or PTSD.
- Project Valour-IT provides voice-controlled laptops and personal GPS systems to service members recovering from hand wounds and other severe injuries including traumatic brain injury and PTSD.
- National Center for Post-Traumatic Stress Disorder provides research and education on trauma and PTSD with a mission to improve the well-being and understanding of individuals who have experienced traumatic events with a focus on American veterans.

Traumatic Brain Injury

- Defense and Veterans Brain Injury Center created the A Head for the Future initiative to raise awareness and lower the risk of concussion. The campaign offers information about the signs, symptoms, and treatment of brain injuries and educates service members and veterans about how to prevent them.
- The Defense Centers of Excellence for Psychological Health and Traumatic Brain Injury provides information and resources about psychological health, post-traumatic stress disorder, or PTSD, and traumatic brain injury.
- Veterans Affairs Polytrauma/Traumatic Brain Injury (TBI) System of Care is an integrated network of specialized rehabilitation programs dedicated to serving veterans and service members with both combat and civilian related TBI and polytrauma.

Online Screening Tools

- Free, confidential, online screenings for anxiety, depression, mood disorders, PTSD, and other conditions are available at http://www. mhascreening.org, Mental Health America's screening service.

National Center for Post-Traumatic Stress Disorder

- The Department of Veteran Affairs website offers a broad range of information about post-traumatic stress disorder and treatment options as well as a VA facilities locator. You may also call (802) 296-6300.

VA's Airborne Hazards and Open Burn Pit Registry

If you were out there burning trash or human shit don't be stupid and register to find out if you have any underlying health concerns.

https://www.publichealth.va.gov/exposures/burnpits/registry.asp

Housing and Homelessness

VASH Program: The HUD-Veterans Affairs Supportive Housing (HUD-VASH) program combines Housing Choice Voucher (HCV) rental assistance for homeless Veterans with case management and clinical services provided by the Department of Veterans Affairs (VA). VA provides these services for participating Veterans at VA medical centers (VAMCs) and community-based outreach clinics.

SSVF: Under the SSVF program, VA awards grants to private non-profit organizations and consumer cooperatives who can provide supportive services to very low-income Veteran families living in or transitioning to permanent housing. Grantees provide eligible Veteran families with outreach, case management, and assistance in obtaining VA and other benefits, which may include:
Health care services
- Daily living services
- Personal financial planning services

- Transportation services
- Fiduciary and payee services
- Legal services
- Childcare services
- Housing counseling services

Homeless Veteran Stand Downs: Stand Downs are typically one- to three-day events providing supplies and services such as food, shelter, clothing, health screenings, and VA Social Security benefits counseling to homeless Veterans. Veterans can also receive referrals to other assistance such as health care, housing solutions, employment, substance use treatment and mental health counseling. Stand Downs are collaborative events, coordinated between local VA Medical Centers, other government agencies and community-based homeless service providers.

National Coalition for Homeless Veterans: The National Coalition for Homeless Veterans (NCHV) is the resource and technical assistance center for a national network of community-based service providers and local, state and federal agencies that provide emergency and supportive housing, food, health services, job training and placement assistance, legal aid, and case management support for hundreds of thousands of homeless veterans each year.

Employment

VA Vocational Rehabilitation and Employment Home: Veterans may receive vocational rehabilitation and employment services to help with job training, employment, resume development, and job-seeking skills coaching. Other services may be provided to assist Veterans in starting their own businesses or independent living services for those who are severely disabled and unable to work in traditional employment.

VA Employment Programs for Homeless Veterans: VA's Compensated Work Therapy (CWT) Program is a national vocational program comprised of three unique programs that assist homeless Veterans in returning to competitive employment: Sheltered Workshop, Transitional Work, and Supported Employment. Veterans in CWT are paid at least the federal or state minimum wage, whichever is higher.

American Job Centers: America's Service Locator connects individuals to employment and training opportunities available at local American Job Centers. The website provides contact information for a range of local work-related services, including unemployment benefits, career development, and educational opportunities.

National Veterans Foundation Job Board: A listing of jobs across the country at companies interesting in hiring veterans.

Work for Warriors (Guard and Reserve): Job Postings & Unit Vacancies. The California Military Department is a diverse, community-based organization comprised of four pillars: the California Army National Guard, the California Air National Guard, the California State Military Reserve, and the California Youth and Community Programs.

Small Business (SBA Veteran & Disabled Veterans): If you are a veteran or service-disabled veteran, SBA has resources to help you start and grow your small business.

Health

VA Care Providers Program: For Caregivers of Veterans. "VA values your commitment as a partner in our pledge to care for those who have 'borne the battle,' and we have several support and service options designed with you in mind. The programs are available both in and out of your home to help you care for the Veteran you love and for yourself."

Addiction

SAMHSA: The Substance Abuse and Mental Health Services Administration (SAMHSA) is the agency within the US Department of Health and Human Services that leads public health efforts to advance the behavioral health of the nation. SAMHSA's mission is to reduce the impact of substance abuse and mental illness on America's communities. SAMHSA leads efforts to ensure that American servicemen and women and their families can access behavioral health treatment and services. For Addiction Support 24/7 Call SAMHSA: 800-662-4357 (HELP).

Addiction Resource: Veterans and Substance Abuse: The Many Sides of the Problem - Addiction Resource was founded in 2014 to provide a community for those recovering from addiction and to help patients find the highest quality care for a successful recovery. Their goal is to provide resources to help patients and their loved ones so that they may stay on the road to recovery and can successfully overcome addiction for life.

Social Support

The Mission Continues: "The Mission Continues empowers veterans facing the challenge of adjusting to life at home to find new missions. We redeploy veterans in their communities so that their shared legacy will be one of action and service. Through the Mission Continues, veterans serve their country in new ways by engaging in our innovative and action-oriented programs. The first, The Mission Continues' Fellowship, harnesses veterans' strengths, skills, and their compassion and empowers them to volunteer with non-profit organizations in their community on a daily basis. The second, The Mission Continues' Service Platoons, brings teams of veterans who are working together with partners at the local level to build stronger communities and tackle pressing issues."

Team Red, White, and Blue: "Team RWB's mission is to enrich the lives of America's veterans by connecting them to their community through physical and social activity."

Iraq and Afghanistan Veterans of America (IAVA): "Founded in 2004 by an Iraq veteran at a time when there were little to no resources available for post-9/11 vets, Iraq and Afghanistan Veterans of America (IAVA) has quickly become the nation's largest nonprofit, nonpartisan organization representing new veterans and their families. Now, with nearly 300,000 veterans and civilian supporters nationwide, IAVA is the only 21st Century veterans' service organization (VSO) dedicated to standing with the 2.8 million veterans of Iraq and Afghanistan from their first day home through the rest of their lives."

Team Rubicon: "Team Rubicon unites the skills and experiences of military veterans with first responders to rapidly deploy emergency response teams."

Student Veterans of America – Mission: "To provide military veterans with the resources, support, and advocacy needed to succeed in higher education and following graduation."

American Legions: "Focusing on service to veterans, servicemembers and communities, The American Legion currently has about 2.4 million members in 14,000 posts worldwide."

VFW - Veterans of Foreign Wars USA – Mission: "To foster camaraderie among United States veterans of overseas conflicts. To serve our veterans, the military, and our communities. To advocate on behalf of all veterans."

Feed Our Vets: Since 2008, Feed Our Vets has provided free food assistance to more than 20,000 Veterans and their family members, distributing 445,000 lbs. of food. Feed Our Vets mission is to help Veterans in the United States, their spouses and children, whose circumstances have left them on the battlefield of hunger,

Next Step Service Dogs - Mission: "to empower positive change for veterans with invisible disabilities such as Post-Traumatic Stress Disorder (PTSD) and Traumatic Brain Injury (TBI) through the use of expertly-trained service dogs."

Veterans Moving Forward: They provide service dogs to veterans with physical and behavioral health concerns.

Veterans Legal Institute: "Veterans Legal Institute (VLI) seeks to provide pro bono legal assistance to homeless and low income current and former service members so as to eradicate barriers to housing, education, employment and healthcare and foster self-sufficiency."

National Veterans Legal Services Program (NVLSP): "The NVLSP is a nonprofit organization that has worked since 1980 to ensure that the government delivers to our nation's 25 million veterans and active duty personnel the benefits to which they are entitled because of disabilities resulting from their military service to our country."

Transportation

Recycled Rides™: a military/veteran support program designed to help ease the transportation burden for current military and veterans. They provide refurbished vehicles to deserving recipients. Their technicians restore these vehicles to proper driving condition.

Acknowledgments

To my wife, I probably would not have even written this book without your help and dedication to push me through the hurdles. Your constant pursuit of my mental health was always your number one priority. Numerous times, you had to force me to call and make appointments to see doctors for various of reasons, with the only objective to get me help. I was depressed and lost coming back from that second deployment and although the job kept me busy throughout the years of field rotations and leadership positions, the past two and a half years seem to have been the roughest. I think that is why I am finally starting to put my thoughts on paper and publish this book because I have noticed a change in my mental health. I have not been the same person and almost feel mentally and emotionally absent. For two years, I have been completely lost and it was you, still holding my hand and guiding me through the fog. I finally feel that I can start my recovery process and find myself again.

To my family, I hope that finally after all these years, this provides a small amount of detail. Although I didn't always tell you things that happened in Afghanistan I hope this may open your eyes to a few days I had, but it definitely isn't everything. Thank you for building my foundation during my childhood and through some tough times, supporting me from a far. I miss all of you so much and I wish I could live closer and not miss out on so much.

This book would not be possible without the efforts of so many people, some I know I may forget, and I truly apologize. I've crossed many paths and connected with so many walks of life. I mean no disrespect if I misspelled or forgotten your name. Believe me, if you ever walked into my life, and there are rarely people that have negatively walked out, I appreciate your friendship.

To all my soldiers, God I miss you guys. I think about all of you, even though I may not call or reach out like I should. Although sometimes I failed, just know you and your family were always at my mind's forefront. I wouldn't be where I am without your efforts. I would gladly give my life for any of you, if given the opportunity. Though our paths crossed for a short time, I hope you all grow into great leaders, regardless if you are in the military or not.

To all of my mentors, thank you for taking a chance with me. Thank you for the long talks and the harsh realities. Thank you for always putting others before yourself and show me hard right over the easy left. Long counseling sessions, hard smoke sessions and constant corrective training were the small building blocks to my future leadership style. You all taught me to go out and not try and build the biggest and best leadership wall. You taught me to place a brick as perfectly as a brick can be laid and soon enough you will have a wall. Thank you for all of the life lessons.

I wish nothing but the best for all of you and I hope you all find peace in life.

Aaron Kozloff
Adam Pleasants
Aimee Ambriz
Alexander Chapman
Alexander Cornelius
Alexander Paquin
Amanda Embry
Andres Villavencia
Andrew Bossi
Andrew Gluekert
Andrew McIntire
Andrew Schaffer
Angel Garcia
Angel Mendoza
Anthony Dement
Anthony Romeo
Antwan Taylor
Ashleigh Grue
Ashley Spooner
Axel Castellanos
Ben Cranson
Ben Hildring
Benjamin Byerly
Benjamin Guerrero
Berry Oakes
Billy Tull
Bradley Bray
Brandon Chatman
Brandon Lee
Brandon Systo
Brandon Weinlein
Brantley Bub
Brent Brian

Brent Cushing
Brian Gentry
Brian Goldman
Brian Gulden
Brooke Spencer
Bryan Gutierrez
Bub Brantley
Carissa LePage
Carl Bell
Cassi Rodeheaver
Cera Wood
Chaz Favier
Chelsea Poterfield
Cheyenne Bangle
Cheyenne Selbe
Christopher Justus
Christopher Luoma
Christin Patrick
Christina Malloy
Christine Juarez
Christopher Cordova
Christopher Fifeld
Christopher Heberer
Christopher Housel
Christopher Lee
Christopher Melton
Christopher Mendes
Christopher Silva
Cindy Lisbon
CJ DuTart
Claire Cox
Clark Brubaker
Cody Reuterskiold

Connor Stark
Cornelius Frazier
Courtney Williams
Craig Lyle
Craig Wallace
Curtis Lewis
Dakota Layne
Dameon Skaggs
Daniel Barber
Daniel Gotschall
Daniel Parten
Dashonn Fleming
Dave Padilla
David Beaton
David Grulke
David Haskins
David Howard
David Kenner
David Ley
David Mihalsky
David Valenzuela
Deja Polk
Dennisalvin David
Derian Moore
Dimir Brown
Dominic Stephens-
  Olson
Donell Roberts
Donovan McManus
Dorothy Hunter
Duane Garrison
Dustin Doyle
Dylan Racine

Dylan Velez	JaRoyce Mason	Joseph Sherbino
Eric Dugan	Jason Jasinski	Joseph Willie
Erik Hamza	Jason Kaack	Josh Longoria
Erika Bienlien	Jason Kercheski	Joshua Hayhurst
Ethan Ferral	Jason Michel	Joshua Jordan
Fabian Diaz	Jay Gelinas	Joshua Longoria
Fragile Ealey	Jefferey Sadker	Joshua Powell
Frank Lew	Jeffery Shultz	Julian Marcano
Gabrielle Lahti	Jenifer Tauzin	Justin Bemis
Garrett Banks	Jennifer Amundson	Justin Bixler
Gary O'Neil	Jeremy Gross	Justin Johnson
Gilbert Guzman	Jeremy Hollenbach	Justin Riling
Grant Cook	Jeremy Kiel	Justin Ring
Grant Sullivan	Jeremy Mijaromero	Karl Moore
Gregory Holmes	Jeremy Shepard	Kathy Rothenberger
Gustavo Hernandez	Jeremy Weller	Katie Casper
Haley Anderson	Jesse Leon	Keanan Kite
Hayden Egeland	Jessica Markley	Keisha McCaig
Heath Phillips	Jessica Serrano	Keith Kureska
Henry Spruill	Jim Lane	Kevin Michigan
Heriberto Hernandez	Joe Carter	Kevin Smiley
Hollie McLane	Joel Dominguez	Kevin Tam
Ian Strook	Joey Dela Cruz	Kevin Wood
Isabel Vasquez	John Wall	Kyle Bates
Israel Thompson	Johnathan Rivera	Kylie Wynn
Jacob Hiemstra	Johnathan Sterns	Luke Eagan
Jacob Kellner	Jon Ringwell	Marcos Orozco
Jacob Sanchez	Jon Waterhouse	Marcus Bennett
Jakob Reed	Jonathan Ciarrone	Marcus Brown
James Belton	Jonathan Denton	Mark Ellsion
James Breckinridge	Jonathan Narcisse	Marquise Morton
James Camba	Jonathan Yasuda	Matt Nowak
James Strong	Joseph Brosenne	Matthew Crawford

Matthew Elam
Matthew Joy
Matthew Negoshi
Matthew Nowak
Maximillian Waring
Michael Buyno
Michael Burgos
Michael Dills
Michael Gieger
Michael Grant
Michael Hajworonsky
Michael Hayes
Michael Hayslett
Michael Higginbotham
Michael Jaimes
Michael Johnson
Michael Matthews
Michael McGonigal
Michael Stevens
Michael Toledo
Michael Truitt
Michael Vaughn
Michael Verillo
Michael Wiegel
Mike McLean
Mischa Turner
Molly DuTart
Natasha Kesterson
Nicholas Cox
Nicholas Schroeder
Nicolas Guiterrez

Niki Lopez
Nikol Domengeaux
Nina Viega
Nolan Alberg
Omar Calo
Oscar Sainz
Patrick Christian
Quinten Epting
Raymond Muckelroy
Richard LeClair
Rick Souza
Robert Poterfield
Robert Sepulveda
Rodney Rodriguez
Ruth Baez
Ryan Eberhard
Ryan Patsky
Ryan Rivas
Sam Koch
Samuel Matlock
Samuel Vaught
Sarah McManus
Scott Luellman
Scott Sobataka
Scott Taylor
Sean John
Sean Thomas
Sequoia Sims
Shane Jarzynka
Shawn Bruner
Shianne Winters
Stephan Mace
Terell Barnes

Terence Darby
Teresa Duncan
Thomas Hughes
Timothy Coon
Todd Anderson
Tom Tienda
Tony Anderson
Torrance Polk
Tracey Jacobson
Tracy Northington
Travis Nicholson
Tristen Crowell
Trong Nguyen
Tyler Grier
Tyler Harmon
Tyler Parten
Vincent "Rocco" Vargas
Vistor Ortiz
Wileen Becker
William Duran
William Threadgill
William Richie
Zachary Exline
Zachary Goehler
Zachary Kountz
Zachary Leija
Zachary Richmond
Zachary Robinson
Zachary Stergiades

MENTOR MILITARY
FOR THE MILITARY PROFESSIONAL

Why Shop from **MentorMilitary.com?**

- Our product selection is curated specifically for servicemembers

- Competitive pricing, our prices are often beat Amazon

- Most orders ship within 1 business day

- We ship to APO/FPOs

- We offer a 30-Day Money Back Guarantee on our books

Books, Software, and Tools to Accelerate your Military Career
Visit MentorMilitary.com

Do You Want to be
Published?

- Want to become one of our authors or subject matter experts?

- Do you have a manuscript you'd like to see published?

- Have an idea for a product you want to pitch?

- **Send us a message. Your budding idea might be a new bestseller!**

We publish for all services:
Army, Air Force, Navy, and Marines
Email us: admin@mentorinc.us

MENTOR MILITARY
FOR THE MILITARY PROFESSIONAL

Books, Software, Mobile Apps, and Tools to Accelerate your Military Career
Visit MentorMilitary.com